SPEAKING FR

SPEAKING FROM THE HOLY LAND

LANCE R. SHILTON,

B.A., B.D., Th.L.
Rector of Holy Trinity Church
Adelaide, South Australia

Foreword by
The Most Rev. Marcus L. Loane, M.A., D.D., Th.D.,
Archbishop of Sydney

OLIPHANTS

OLIPHANTS

BLUNDELL HOUSE
GOODWOOD ROAD
LONDON S.E.14

*The poem on p. 101 Today Thou shalt be with
me by Studdert Kennedy is reproduced by per-
mission of Hodder and Stoughton Limited.*

ISBN 0 551 00187 9

Made and printed in Great Britain by
Willmer Brothers Limited, Birkenhead
and C. Tinling & Co. Ltd., Prescot, Lancs.

FOREWORD

In this book, the author has made skilful and interesting use of his experience as a visitor to "those holy fields" where the Son of Man walked in the midst of men. The initial chapter starts with Qumran and provides a basis for all that follows in a clear statement on the authority of the Word of God. The other chapters move from Bethlehem to Galilee, following the order of our Lord's life from His birth to His death, and reaching a climax with His Resurrection and the outpoured gift of the Holy Ghost on the Day of Pentecost. The great historic sites of old Palestine are used as a door that opens the way to an exposition of the Gospel, and the result clearly shows how the Land throws light on the Word, and how the Word throws light on the Lord. I am glad to commend this book to all into whose hands it may come.

MARCUS L. LOANE

CONTENTS

DEDICATED TO
MY DAUGHTERS
PAULINE AND ANDREA

PREFACE

This book was ready for publication prior to the explosive six-day Middle East War of June, 1967; I have made some necessary alterations since then. By the time the book is published the political situation may have changed again, as it has done many times through the centuries, but the basic spiritual appeal of the Holy Land will always remain the same.

Each chapter deals with a place made significant by the coming of the Son of Man. Because the Gospel of Christ is always relevant, I have endeavoured to apply to our situation today what was said and done so long ago.

I am grateful to all who have assisted in the compilation of the book, and to those from whose writings quotations have been made. I regret that in some cases I have not been able to trace their sources.

My sincere prayer is that this book will bring many to a personal faith in Christ, "who for us men and for our salvation . . . was made man".

L.R.S.

1   EXAMINING THE RECORDS

Every child in Sunday School has heard how a shepherd boy threw some pebbles with a wonderful intent and purpose—that of freeing his people from the threats of an overweening giant (1 Sam. 17). "Thou comest to me with a sword" said David to Goliath, "and with a spear, and with a shield; but I come to thee in the name of the Lord of hosts, the God of the armies of Israel, whom thou hast defied" (v. 45). Thousands of years later, another shepherd boy, without any conscious purpose, tossed pebbles into a cave on the shores of the Dead Sea.

His action was aimless—just a way of amusing himself when there was nothing else to do. But when a pebble struck against something in the darkness there, something which gave off a metallic sound, he was moved to something more purposeful. Could there be treasure in that place?

Treasure there was indeed! and although the lad may have been disappointed when all that was brought to light turned out to be some old scrolls, he doubtless did recover his earlier interest and pleasure when these scrolls rivetted the attention of the learned world (and scholars were prepared to pay heavily for them!)

Ever since that day Bedouins and archaeologists have been searching every hole and crevice of that wild and desolate area. These discoveries have been the most outstanding in modern times; Biblical manuscripts 2,000 years old, and of prime importance, not only for the authenticity of the Biblical text, but also for the historicity of Christianity. Here is unveiled part of the background against which the teaching of Jesus and the constitution of the early Church arose.

Members of the Essene community lived in caves and huts along the cliff. At the foot of the rugged cliff, looking towards the Dead Sea and the mountains of Moab, I saw the ruins of an ancient monastery. In these haunting hostile surroundings, several hundred "Brothers" spent their life under strict rules of poverty, studying the Holy Writings and praying for the coming of the Messiah.

It was one of the most unforgettable journeys of my life—from the shores of the Dead Sea to Qumran, a thirty minute journey in an Arab-driven taxi through rough country, passing over-turned, rusting tanks used in the Israeli-Jordan war of 1948. The red glow of the setting sun was on the heavy, salt-saturated, lifeless sea. Dust from the bare hills and sand-covered mounds blew in my face, but I persevered across the narrow ridges of a rocky cliff and crawled into the tiny cave.

Later, at the Palestine Archaeological Museum in Jerusalem, I looked with amazement at the oldest manuscripts of the Old Testament in existence. Altogether, remains of more than 600 different manuscripts have been found in eleven caves in the Qumran region. They date from the third century B.C. to A.D. 68. According to the Curator of the Museum, they contain fragments, large and small, of every book of the

Old Testament except Esther, a curious and perhaps accidental omission. Most are written in Hebrew, but there are also works in Aramaic and a few in Greek.

When I thought of the desolate ruins in the Dead Sea wilderness and saw these precious ancient Scriptures I thought of words of the prophet Isaiah, which they contained: "Surely the people is grass. The grass withereth, the flower fadeth: but the word of our God shall stand for ever" (Isaiah 40:7, 8).

Forty men, or thereabouts, wrote the Bible's sixty six books over a period of one thousand six hundred years. They spoke different languages, they lived in different countries, and in different times. But their message is one message. God spoke to each man in his own language and in his own time, but the message was basically the same. When scholars gathered together the many ancient manuscripts of the Old and New Testaments, written in Hebrew, Aramaic and Greek, and translated into a single, modern tongue, they found that God's promises remained unchanged. His great message to man had not varied. So it is today, that as we read these words, we find them full of meaning for this twentieth century. No wonder that the Bible has always been one of the world's best sellers. The Bible is unique as the written record of the revelation of God made to us in Christ. From the Bible we get our knowledge of God and His will, and through the Bible we obtain all the light and guidance we need to live the Christian life. But we must approach it in the right way.

We must accept it confidently. Gladstone called the Bible "the impregnable rock of Holy Scripture". The authority of scripture is not a matter to be defended so much as to be asserted. Charles Spurgeon once said, "There's no need for you to defend a lion when he's being attacked. All you need to do is open the gate and let him out".

The Scriptures themselves claim authority. They come to us as the Word of God. The phrases, "The Lord said", "the Lord spake", "the Word of the Lord came", are used 3,808 times in the Old Testament. The writers make it clear that these words do not spring from their own ideas nor from their insight. They believed themselves to be uttering the oracles of the Living God.

Christ Himself fully accepted this, and often said, "It is written". This was how He met the attack of Satan at the time of His temptation, saying, "It is written."

The New Testament contains many quotations from the Old: a specific and explicit statement in the New Testament with regard to the character of the Old Testament is found in II Timothy 3:16: "All Scripture is given by inspiration of God, and is profitable for doctrine, for reproof, for correction, for instruction in righteousness". Peter explained, "No prophecy ever came by the impulse of man, but men moved by the Holy Spirit spoke from God" (II Pet. 1:21, RSV). Many before us have accepted the Bible confidently and found it trustworthy; so too may we.

We must use it intelligently. While it is true that some have found help by opening the Bible at random and reading what first came to their eyes, it is certainly not an intelligent way of finding guidance: it is so easy to take a text out of its context and apply it wrongly. No one would think of trying to understand

Shakespeare's plays, or a scientific textbook, in that way.

Here are some general rules for Bible study:

1. Look for the true meaning of words, taking them in their common or usual sense, in which their original hearers or readers would have understood them.

2. It is most important to be certain whether a particular passage is literal or figurative. A passage may be fact or fiction, history or allegory, prose or poetry, narrative or discourse.

3. Chapter or other divisions, or chapter headings do not form part of the original and may be misleading.

4. Interpret in relation to the context. "A text without a context is a pretext".

5. Interpret grammatically.

6. Steer between taking the words over-literally, and treating everything as an analogy of something "hidden".

7. Interpret the Old Testament in the light of the New Testament.

8. Compare Scripture with Scripture and let Scripture check one's interpretation of Scripture.

9. Recognize the inevitable paradoxes since we deal with infinite things, and be prepared to accept both extremes, such as the sovereignty of God and the freewill of man.

10. Interpret the obscure by the clear. It is wrong to take the measure of our own understanding as a standard for deciding the meaning, or judging the value, of Scripture. What a ridiculous position we would find ourselves in if, in other matters, we refused to accept everything which we could not understand. Most of

us would never switch the light on, for we certainly do not understand electricity!

11. Respect the judgment of others. It is dangerous for anyone to imagine that he has a monopoly of truth. "If, I found myself being led to a conclusion which is in conflict with some statement in the Apostles' Creed, I ought if I am sensible, to question the accuracy of my own conclusion and be inclined to think that the Creed may be correct, and I mistaken". (T. Russell Howden).

12. Seek the enlightenment of the Holy Spirit. He is the only Teacher fully able to expound His own inspired text book.

We should read the Bible systematically, not just when we may have time to spare, not just when we feel like it, and not only when faced with a sudden emergency.

The Scripture Union has been guiding many millions of people in the systematic reading of the Bible since 1867, and by means of specially prepared notes for all age groups, men and women, boys and girls the world over have come to the knowledge of Christ as Saviour and Lord.

But whatever method you use the important thing is for you to read the Bible, not spasmodically nor superficially, but systematically.

We should use the Bible as our prime guide. Christians are often tempted to substitute some other worthy activity for the reading of God's Word. Visiting Rome and the Art Galleries of Florence, or even travelling to the Holy Land, is not a substitute for the reading of the Word of God. Gregory, Bishop of Nyssa, far back in A.D. 380, said something we should ponder. "Before I ever saw Jerusalem, I knew that Christ was Very God. I knew that God was born of a virgin before I saw Bethlehem's stable. I believed in the Lord's resurrection before I looked upon the church built upon its memory. This little profit alone did I get for my journey."

For this early Christian, travel was no substitute for Bible reading.

It is so easy for ministers, Sunday School teachers, youth leaders, church officers and others, to neglect the study of the Word of God, and to put other things in its place. It is not sufficient to read books about the Bible, or to listen to someone else reading the Bible on a radio service, or a telecast: we must read it ourselves, and it should have a priority in our reading. It is not just another book: it is God's Book, and its message is relevant to everyman today.

Five times our Lord asked a question of different groups of religious leaders, simple in itself, but full of import: "Have ye not read?" He twice asked the Pharisees this; twice the Chief Priests and Scribes, and once the Sadducees. In these five texts there clearly stands out the basic fact that for Jesus the great questions of life can be answered only from the Word of God.

On these occasions He was talking to the most educated men in Israel. They were able to read the Word of God. No other people on earth at that time had this privilege. Neither the Greeks nor the Romans had any divinely inspired volume. But the ability to read the Word carried the responsibility of understanding it, believing and obeying it. Yet although they could quote hundreds of passages, they had not entered into the deeper implications of many of these revealed truths.

They had constructed a system of error; some were ethically insincere, and all were blind to the fact that their Messiah, of whom the Word of God spoke to them, stood in their midst. They did not recognize it because they read the Scriptures, as it were, with eyes blind to the truth of God.

We need to approach the Word of God reverently, for it contains the message of Jesus Christ, our Saviour. He is the theme of the Old and the New Testaments.

Simple, clear, bold, is this message of the Living Son of God. It is the message of Jesus Christ, and it contains His offer of peace with God. We must listen to the Word of God obediently, for Jesus said that we must hear the Word, and do it. Then we shall come into complete certainty, as Augustine did in the early centuries.

In his youth Augustine was wild and reckless, given over to riotous living and drunkenness. He went through a time of heart-searching, when he realized that he was a sinner before God. Then one day he heard a voice saying, "Take up and read. Take up and read". He took up a New Testament that was lying there and read Romans 13, verse 13, "Let us walk honestly, as in the day; not in rioting and drunkenness, not in chambering and wantonness, not in strife and envying. But put ye on the Lord Jesus Christ, and make not provision for the flesh".

Augustine says in his Confessions, "No further would I read, nor need I. For instantly at the end of this sentence, by a light, as it were, of serenity infused into my heart, all the darkness of doubt vanished away". He heard the Word and obeyed it.

If then we read God's Word in these ways we shall

find our way to Jesus Christ, the Son of God, and we shall receive glad assurance of the forgiveness of our sins, the certainty of our salvation, and the commission to make these great things known to others.

2   LET US GO TO BETHLEHEM

Bethlehem is a name of strong appeal. All over the world, wherever Christian people celebrate Christmas, this name carries its message into human hearts. The town stands six miles south of Jerusalem. I journeyed along the road where Israelites and Philistines, Egyptians, Assyrians, Babylonians, Greeks, Romans and Persians, Moslem invaders and Crusader liberators, Saracens and Turks, and later troops of Britain had marched in their day. Abraham drove his sheep this way to Hebron: Samuel, the prophet, visited the house of Jesse to find David who roamed these hills and plains guarding his sheep from the attack of lion and bear. Rehoboam trod this road to build a fortress at Bethlehem, David's royal city. When Caesar Augustus would enrol the world, it was hither that Joseph and Mary came.

Bethlehem is a city set on a hill. It is a peaceful and attractive little town, with white, flat-roofed houses nestling close together. Nearby is the Shepherds' field where humble men heard the angels of heaven sing, "Glory to God in the Highest". The visitor is taken to a cave where it is claimed that the shepherds slept. On the top of the hill you see a small belfry over the church which contains the famous Bells of Bethlehem which ring round the world on Christmas Day. Many times each day a piercing loud call from the mosque reminds the Moslems who live there that it is time to pray. Eventually you make your way to the Church of the Holy Nativity through numerous would-be sales-men who offer "cheap" souvenirs carved in mother-of-pearl, Holy Land flowers, postcards and stamps. This church, built probably in A.D. 330 by Queen Helena, mother of Constantine, the first Christian Emperor of Rome, is the oldest church in the world still used for worship, and the only one which has survived Palestine's innumerable invasions. In A.D. 611 the Persians destroyed every Christian church in Palest-ine except this one. When they reached Bethlehem, intent upon pillage and destruction, they saw pictures of themselves at its entrance, in glorious mosaics! The wise men, bowing before the infant Christ, were clad in Persian dress so they entered the church and wor-shipped also.

You enter by a low door. Some tell you that this is so that you will be forced to bow your head in ador-ation; others say it was to prevent the Moslems riding in on horseback and slaying the worshippers; yet others, to prevent travellers taking their beasts inside and making it a lodging place. Traces of older door-ways can be seen in the surrounding stonework.

The Church, a cold, austere Roman basilica, with massive Corinthian pillars and gold mosaics still discernible on the walls, is a not unpleasing building. For a reasonable tip a guide will open a large trap-door in the floor of the nave, and as you peer down you will notice extensive remains of the mosaic floor of the original cave or grotto. You descend one or two narrow stairways, with steps which are worn down by innumerable pilgrims. You stand in silence before a shrine which has a silver star set in marble. The low roof of irregular rock is blackened with age and the smoke of endless candles. The air is heavy with incense. The place is lighted by dozens of lamps tended by priests. Down three more steps a tiny chapel commemorates the situation of the manger and the place where it is said the wise men knelt to adore the infant Christ.

The words of the Latin inscription near the Star of Bethlehem remain in your mind, "This is where Jesus Christ was born of the Virgin Mary".

Christianity is based on a life lived in places which still may be visited. The critic may argue as he likes, and use the division of Christendom as the object of his easy scorn; but in one thing all churches agree. A human life was begun at Bethlehem which offers to all men the key to the problems of their lives. The facts of the gospel story have been subjected to the most rigid criticism and enquiry. The light of nearly 2,000 years of scholarship has beaten upon them, and not only do they bear the scrutiny, but from these pages leaps the figure of a living Man. No wonder the hymnwriter said,

> "O come, all ye faithful,
> Joyful and triumphant;
> O come ye, O come ye to Bethlehem".

Having examined the place *where* Jesus was born, now let us consider the time *when* Jesus was born.

The story of Christmas (says Leon Morris) is the story of the most stupendous happening in the history of the world, for it is the story of God sending His Son to earth. It is the story of God's action for man's salvation, for Bethlehem leads right on to Calvary—a story which runs throughout the pages of the Old Testament as holy men set forth the way of God in law and psalm and history. It takes in the ancient sacrifices which taught that "without shedding of blood is no remission" (Heb. 9:22). It may be traced through the writings of the prophets who, in a variety of expressions, brought out the significance of the coming Messiah. But in the course of time the voice of prophecy fell silent. For four centuries there lacked a voice which could cry "Thus saith the Lord", and to the men of Herod's day it might well have seemed that God had forgotten to be gracious. The Roman Emperor was supreme. His might went unchallenged. Mockers said that God either could not or would not visit His people. Yet the men of that day were on the threshold of seeing the mightiest of all God's mighty acts. He had before sent prophets, but never before had He sent His Son.

Four hundred silent years is a long time, quite long enough for men to begin to think that God will never again do such mighty things as he did in days gone by. But whenever men begin to think like that they are wrong.

Not until the very eve of the day when God's Son would appear was the silence broken. John the Baptist's rugged voice thundered through the hills of Judaea with urgent command, "Repent ye, for the Kingdom of Heaven is at hand". He was the immediate forerunner of God's promised Messiah.

Later, when Paul wrote to the Galatians he said, 'When the fulness of time was come, God sent forth

23

His Son, made of a woman, made under the law, to redeem them that were under the law, that we might receive the adoption of sons" (Gal. 4:4). The way of the Lord was made ready and people prepared for His coming.

It was the fullness of time because, despite all Rome's wonderful achievements, the Empire has been compared to a body without a soul. Men were "seeking for a spiritual unity which should correspond to a material unity". The Romans could give their subjects good laws, uniform government and military protection, but not a satisfactory religion. A universal empire needed a universal religion. The old Roman religion of abstract virtue had gone down in formalism. It was too cold for human hearts. Moral bankruptcy was imminent. At that time Jesus was born at Bethlehem.

Greek thinkers had been exercised about deep questions concerning the nature of God, man and the universe, and their relations to one another. They discussed the meaning and purpose of human life and how best to live it. Many at that time were disappointed with life. They longed for immortality. They searched for salvation from the oppressive sense of fatalism, from the darkness of death, and from the power of demons. Some turned to Stoicism, some to the lofty spiritualism of Plato's theories, some to scepticism, and some to cold nihilism. Others turned to the mystery cults of the East with their rites of purification, asceticism and self-denial. They appealed to the emotions by mortifications, by fasting, by self-mutilation, by evocative music, by drugs and stimulants. Modern man often uses these ancient methods to satisfy his deep longings but just as unsuccessfully. Then, as now, men felt the need for some transforming and uplifting

24

power. The failure of the best achievements of ancient Greece to satisfy man's desperate search for reality was itself an indication that it was time for Jesus to be born at Bethlehem. The Jews, the Romans and the Greeks had been prepared unwittingly for His Coming, even if they did not understand it.

Now consider the reasons for the birth of Jesus. Christ was born to identify himself with man fully, "The Word was made flesh, and dwelt among us, (and we beheld his glory, the glory as of the only begotten of the Father,) full of grace and truth". (John 1:14).

When you have been to the Holy Land people ask you, "Didn't you find it distressing to see all the commercialism surrounding the holy places and to hear the bickering of the various sects?" I have said, "Yes, but it helped me to appreciate what it must have been like in our Lord's day". He was in the midst of it all. If you have been in the habit of thinking of a Jesus clad in a spotless white robe, standing in some romantic setting, hand stretched out to heal, a visit to these places today will correct the picture. You will remember that God chose that Jesus should be born and live amongst men, in a far-off age when things must have been even worse than they are now; and there will come into your voice a hush of wonder and an exclamation of awe when you next repeat the Creed: "Who for us men and for our salvation *was made man*".

The Son of God brushed shoulders with dirty humanity. He stood up for the rights of those who were wronged. He was tempted in all points as we are, yet without sin. He comforted the sorrowful, He healed the sick, He cleansed the lepers, He welcomed the outcasts, He condemned the hypocrites, He inspired His followers. Christ's birth at Bethlehem was the most

25

effective way for God to show to all men, and to every man, that He is not remote from you and your problems, somewhere above the bright blue sky, but that He cares.

I do not know what your need is at this moment. It may be comfort, for an answer to life's problems, for strength to persevere, for the peace of forgiveness; whatever it is, Christ can meet your need. You cannot have an experience which He does not understand and share. Christ fully identified Himself with man.

Then, too, Christ was born to reveal the love of God clearly. John wrote in his Epistle, "In this was manifested the love of God toward us, because that God sent his only begotten Son into the world, that we might live through him" (1 John 4:9).

This was a different picture from what men had previously believed. Because of the holiness, the righteousness and the severe justice of God man hardly dare approach Him. But the prophets had had a glimmer of the truth when they spoke about God's mercy and love to those who turned to Him. Then Jesus came with the full revelation of God's love and demonstrated once and for all that God, our God, matches His justice with His love and His righteousness with His truth, and will satisfy man's every need.

This love was not shown in a blaze of heavenly glory as might seem fitting for the King of Kings. It was demonstrated in a most humble way. We read that Christ was born in conditions of utter poverty which it is difficult for us to envisage. The inn itself was lowly: yet there was no room even there. It was in a manger that He was laid. All this shows clearly the depth of God's love for us men.

Finally, Christ was born to save sinful man eternally.

"For God so loved the world that he gave his only begotten Son, that whosoever believeth in him should not perish, but have everlasting life" (John 3:16). This well-known text is often called "The Gospel in a nutshell". The essential point is that God took action to deal with the sin of our world, and gave His Son to be our Saviour. When the Son of God came, His mission was to save men from their sins. His very name indicates the central purpose that was before Him, for the name Jesus means "God is Salvation".

Even in the midst of this touching manger scene sin's stark reality appears; we hear of Herod's diabolical scheme to destroy the Babe, involving the slaughter of the Innocents. Christ never appeared to Herod. Herod never came to see Him: but there is a day coming when the Herods of this world will meet Jesus face to face. It will be the Judgment Day. All see Him then. Our eternal destiny will be related to whether or not we have come to Christ before. We should show goodwill towards men, not from sentimental motives, but because we are men for whom Christ lived and died.

The shepherds came to Bethlehem. They came humbly, simply, sincerely. They came in obedience to the direction of God. They came with nothing in their hands. We, too, must first come with nothing in our hands. As the hymn-writer said,

"Just as I am, without one plea,
But that Thy blood was shed for me,
And that Thou bidd'st me come to Thee,
O Lamb of God, I come!"

Then we may come again to Bethlehem: this time

like the Wise Men with gifts in our hands to express our devotion to Him. We may come with our hearts filled with love for Him, putting all that we have at His feet. Then we shall see Jesus, not as humble babe, but as King of Glory. We shall ask the King of Glory to come into our hearts and be born again in our lives. Our pilgrimage to Bethlehem will not be simply the recognition of the One who went all the way to Calvary to take away our sins, but also of the One who now is risen, ascended and reigning in heaven as the King of Kings.

3   ON JORDAN'S BANKS

The Jordan is probably the most famous river in the world. This dreamy, muddy stream is liquid history. Thousands upon thousands of pilgrims over the years have journeyed to plunge into its waters, wearing white gowns which they have taken home to keep for their shrouds.

Not long ago I stood, where myriads have stood before me, beneath the overhanging trees at the place where tradition holds that Jesus was baptised by John. How could I resist putting my hands into that water? I wanted, too, to be baptized with the spiritual baptism with which Christ was baptized, yet realized the deep implications of what I sought.

The Jordan is a weird stream. It is two hundred and thirty-three miles long. It twists and turns from Syria and sweet water sources to the bitter waters of the Dead Sea. Unlike most rivers it is a barrier and not a link. It is not navigable. It forms a natural boundary line.

The Jordan is mentioned frequently both in the Old Testament and the New. Lot chose "all the circle of the Jordan" because "it was well watered every where" (Gen. 13:10). Joshua and all Israel crossed over the

Jordan on dry ground (Jos. 3:17). Gideon, Jephthah, David, Elijah and Elisha were all well acquainted with the river. Naaman the Syrian was ordered by Elisha to go wash in the Jordan seven times, that his leprosy might be cleansed (II Kings 5:10). The Jordan is a symbol of death to self, leading the pilgrim on to the promised land. The old negro spiritual sings: "One more river, and that's the River of Jordan, there's one more river to cross".

Jordan is a symbol of cleansing from sin, leading on to effective witness; a symbol of obedience to the Will of God, leading on to complete victory. Immediately after His baptism Christ was led by the Spirit into the wilderness to be tempted of the devil. During that period of forty days and forty nights of severe testing He proved victorious. Strengthened by the assurance given by God the Father at His Baptism when the voice came from heaven, "This is my beloved Son, in whom I am well pleased" (Matt. 3:17) our Lord was completely victorious in fulfilling God's plan for man's salvation.

The River Jordan will always be associated with John the Baptist, whose mission it was to prepare for the coming of the Messiah and to emphasize the only way by which men might be reconciled to God. He fearlessly preached repentance, faith and obedience.

Someone was once asked, "When is a sermon not a sermon?" The reply came, "Nine times out of ten!" But when we turn to the New Testament, we find that each sermon recorded there hits its mark.

Our Lord's Sermon on the Mount sets out a new code of ethics which has remained unsurpassed. Peter's pentecostal sermon at Jerusalem brought conversion to 3,000 souls in one day. Stephen's defence before

the Jewish Council was so convincing and so convicting
that they stoned him to death. Paul's testimony before
King Agrippa was so persuasive that the king said,
"You almost persuade me to be a Christian". Jesus
said concerning John the Baptist, the preacher-pro-
phet, "Among those that are born of women there is
not a greater prophet than John the Baptist" (Luke
7:28). He was not a reed shaken with every wind of
doctrine. He did not sacrifice truth to sentimentality
falsely called "love". He was not gorgeously clothed
in the soft comforts of this world. He was an ascetic
prophet, but more than a prophet; he was the mes-
senger who prepared the way for the coming of Christ.

Thundering from the lips of this rugged warrior of
truth, there repeatedly sounded the blunt command,
"Repent ye; for the Kingdom of Heaven is at hand"
(Matt. 3:2) His sermons compelled attention.

After four long silent centuries, here once more
was a message for the nation. It was indeed good tidings
that the Kingdom of God was at hand. But it was
a frightening thought for those who believed that every
child of Abraham would have the right to enter the
Kingdom, to realize that they had no better right than
the Gentiles, and that even those who were not children of Abraham might enter. Many had thought that
the Advent of the Messiah would be joy for the Jews
but judgment for the Gentiles. This prophet's emphasis
on repentance implied that the Jews who did not repent would not enter, and the Gentiles who did repent
would enter. It was tantamount to saying that John
had excommunicated the whole nation and that no
one would be re-admitted unless he professed, not
merely sorrow for his sins, but resolution to break from
his sins, and begin a new life. As a token of this solemn

transformation of life, those who repented were plunged into the River Jordan to bury the polluted past, and then made to rise again to newness of life.

Plummer remarks, "Analogies for this symbolized washing have been sought in the levitical purification of the Jews and the fragrant bathings of the Essenes. But there was this marked difference; these purifications and bathings were repeatedly daily, or hourly, if technical pollution was supected, whereas John's baptism was administered only once. It represented a decisive crisis, which, it was assumed, could never be experienced again". The old prophets had called, "Repent ye". John the Baptist alone was commissioned to proclaim, "Repent ye; for the Kingdom of Heaven is at hand" (Matt. 3:2).

John preached so compellingly that many of the Pharisees and Sadducees came to his baptism. but the Baptist met them with a challenge stern and severe, "O generation of vipers, who hath warned you to flee from the wrath to come? Bring forth therefore fruits meet for repentance: and think not to say within yourselves, "We have Abraham to our father": for I say unto you, that God is able of these stones to raise up children unto Abraham" (Matt. 3:7–9).

The same message of repentance is needed today, but often it is those who believe themselves to be within the fold, who object most strongly when told that the first need is to repent.

Professor O. Hallesby in his book, "Religious or Christian?", made this penetrating comment: "When God meets a natural man, living a moral and religious life, we notice that this man employs his religion as his best defence against the Gospel's urgent requirements of repentance and regeneration. None are more bitter

32

and more determined opponents of spiritual awakening and conversion than these self-same religious people who have provided themselves with a morality and a religion which they deem sufficient, the very purpose of which is to prevent any further interference on the part of the Lord".

It's easy to regret our sins, but it's hard to repent. The consequences of our wrong-doing may make us sorry for ourselves, if not for other people. Repentance means that we turn from our sins because they cause sorrow to God. Judas was sorry for his sin of betrayal and in his despair committed suicide. Peter repented of his sin of denial, and in faith turned to Christ for forgiveness.

No one can be reconciled to God without faith. Faith is as much a pre-requisite as repentance. John the Baptist emphasised this. He said to those standing by as Jesus came to him, "Behold the Lamb of God, which taketh away the sin of the world" (John 1:29, 36). Peter also used the word "lamb" in reference to Christ (I Peter 1:18, 19 R.S.V.), "We are ransomed", he said, "with the precious blood of Christ, like that of a lamb without blemish or spot". When Philip encountered the Ethiopian eunuch, the African was reading the passage from Isaiah 53, verses 7 and 8, "He was oppressed, and he was afflicted, yet he opened not his mouth: he is brought as a lamb to the slaughter, and as a sheep before her shearers is dumb, so he openeth not his mouth". The name "lamb" is used frequently in the last book of the Bible, Revelation. Here it speaks of the Lamb which was slain and the blood of the Lamb, in which the white-robed saints have been washed.

The Lamb is a symbol of gentleness and power, of authority and wrath, of victory and control, of worship and deity. The bride of the Lamb is the Church.

In effect, John the Baptist is saying, "Look! There is God's Lamb. He will be sacrificed to take away the sin of the whole world".

No Jew could ever hear Jesus called the Lamb without thinking of Him as the sacrifice and the offering to God whereby atonement is made for the sin of man, and through whom man and God are reconciled. The Passover Lamb was the symbol of deliverance. This was definitely demonstrated in the events which brought the Jews out of Egypt. After the stubborn refusal of Pharaoh to let the people go, the angel of the Lord was to walk throughout the land in the night, slaying the first-born son of every Egyptian home. But before this happened, every Jewish household was to take and kill a lamb; they were to dip a branch of hyssop in the blood of the lamb, and with it they were to smear the doorposts of their houses, and when the avenging angel saw the mark, he would pass over that house. To think of Jesus as the Passover Lamb is to see in Him the delivering and rescuing power of God come to earth for the salvation of men. Just as the first Passover Lamb was the sign of God's deliverance of His people from their slavery in Egypt, so Jesus, the second Passover Lamb, is the symbol of their deliverance from slavery to sin and Satan. Yet the lamb was more than a symbol. It was the means of deliverance. The death of the lamb was essential; the blood must be shed and thus the deliverance provided.

To see Jesus as the Lamb at all is to see Him in terms of sacrifice. He is the culmination of the whole sacrificial system of the Old Testament. The writer to the

34

Hebrews saw Him as the sacrifice which makes all other sacrifices unnecessary for ever

Christina Rossetti expressed this clearly in her great hymn.

"None other Lamb, none other Name,
　　None other hope in heaven or earth or sea,
　None other hiding place from guilt and shame,
　　　None beside Thee.

My faith burns low, my hope burns low;
　　Only my heart's desire cries out in me,
　By the deep thunder of its want and woe,
　　　Cries out to Thee."

So many people tell me in the course of counselling that their faith is weak. I tell them that it can be made strong only by exercise. Let the flickering faith which burns low in the lamp of your soul signal its need to God's heart of love.

It is because Christ took upon Himself our iniquities that they are taken away from all those who believe in Him. Potentially the benefits of Christ's sacrifice extend to the whole world, but actually they apply only to those who behold Him in faith.

Christianity is more than a code of ethics; it is more than simply following a good example; it is more than being nice, as some might seek to make this great text read, "God is nice and in Him is no nastiness at all". Christianity is a blood religion; it has a sacrificial system, and it requires personal faith and identification. Before anyone can become a Christian he must heed the words of Christ's forerunner, John the Baptist, and say, "O Lamb of God, that takest away the sin

35

of the world, have mercy upon me".

John's message has a third dimension. As well as repentance towards God and faith in Christ, there is obedience and service. A question arose amongst some of John's disciples. They wondered why so many were coming to Jesus instead of John. The Baptist replied, "you need no teachers to meet your difficulty. The zeal which you display is shown to be mistaken if you only recall what I said. When I announced my mission I declared it to be provisional. No word of mine can have given occasion to the error whereby you claim for me the highest place" (Westcott).

John says he is like the best man at a wedding. He certainly is not the bridegroom, but he wants to do everything he can to help him.

In biblical times it was the privilege of the friend of the bridegroom to prepare everything for the due reception of the bride and the bridegroom. John the Baptist had fulfilled his office in preparing and bringing the representatives of the spiritual Israel, the new divine Bride, to Christ the Bridegroom.

The Apostle John records the words of the Baptist (John 3:29, 30), "He that hath the bride is the bridegroom: but the friend of the bridegroom, which standeth and heareth him, rejoiceth greatly because of the bridegroom's voice: this my joy therefore is fulfilled. He must increase, but I must decrease".

This must be the relationship of every Christian to Christ. He should say, "He must increase, but I must decrease". The worldly principle is, "I must increase". I must increase my business. I must increase my popularity. I must increase my security. I must increase my bank balance. I must increase my acceptance with others. I must increase my influence. But if Christ is to increase in me, I must decrease in myself.

So many Christians try to maintain their Christian lives in an atmosphere of compromise. They want Christ for respectability, security and comfort, and they want the world for popularity, entertainment and conformity. There was a time when Christians gave things up for Christ's sake. They were misunderstood. They gave up pictures, dancing, drinking, smoking; their money, and they gave their time. Now the swing has gone the other way—nothing is to be given up. The half-Christian doesn't want to give anything up. He wants to go on living in the same old way. He doesn't want to decrease, nor to have Christ increase. But to remain in a state of compromise or disobedience means of necessity, whether we recognize it or not, that Christ does decrease.

The obedient Christian is contantly asking how he may decrease as Christ increases.

C. T. Studd, a great pioneer missionary, once said, "If Jesus Christ be God and died for me, then no sacrifice is too great for me to make for Him".

In all my Christian service, I must refrain from acting for self-glorification or recognition, so that Christ may increase and I may decrease. In all my personal evangelism I must be careful that the new Christian does not become too personally attached to me. In all my witness I must stand fearlessly for the truth and not consider my own popularity. I must seek to help others in need and give less attention to my own needs. I must do all to the glory of God. This will demand absolute obedience from me in all I think, do and say. True obedience springs from love.

A love far greater than the measure of man's mind.

"The love which came down at Christmas.
The love which was poured out on the Cross.
The love which conquered death.
The love which is eternal."

The love which requires our personal response in
the terms of the message of John the Baptist: repentance towards God the Father, faith in Christ the
Saviour, and obedience to the Holy Spirit, the strength-
ener.

4   HEALING AT CAPERNAUM

Would you like to come with me to Capernaum? It
is on the north-west shore of the Sea of Galilee. How
different it is now from what it was in Christ's day!
Jesus made it "His own city". At one time it was a
busy thriving town of some fifteen thousand inhabitants. Here Greek, Roman and Jewish civilizations met.
Here beside the lake was a mixture of noise and silence,
wealth and poverty, asceticism and prostitution. Jesus
hinted at this when He said, "And thou, Capernaum,
which are exalted to heaven, shalt be thrust down to
hell" (Luke 10:15).

Today, only the ruins of the synagogue remain,
and these are second century—possibly a recon-
struction of the synagogue which Jesus knew. It has
been partially restored in recent years. Carved on much
of the stone work are not only the familiar Jewish
emblems of the vine, the six-pointed Star of David
(made up of intersecting triangles), the five-pointed
Star of Solomon, the olives, seven-branched candlesticks
and trumpets, but also Roman, pagan emblems; a myth-
ical sea horse, Tritons, even a little temple on wheels,
said to be a reproduction of the Ark of the Covenant,
and on one doorway the Roman eagle itself, suggest-
ing a Roman hand in the building.

There is a good deal of uncertainty as to whether or not this is the actual situation of the original Capernaum; but at least we may say that round about this area some of the mightiest works of the Son of God were done. Here Christ's burning compassion was demonstrated in a variety of ways. He brought purpose to the lives of Peter and Andrew as He called them from their fishing to follow Him, and to Matthew as He called him from the receipt of custom. He brought healing to the centurion's servant, peace to the woman with a haemorrhage, new life to Jairus's daughter. He brought relief to the maniac, vision to the blind, restoration to the man with the withered hand.

Visit Capernaum today and you will be shown what they believe to be the site of Peter's house; Mark tells us that Jesus stayed there. Here Jesus healed Peter's wife's mother. It is an octagonal enclosure with a few mosaics within it, possibly the remains of a fourth century church of Byzantine type. There would be many who had seen or heard about the wonderful things Jesus had done. Luke tells us that "as He was teaching, there were Pharisees and doctors of the Law sitting by, which were come out of every town of Galilee, and Judaea, and Jerusalem" (Luke 5:17). It was perhaps to this place that the four men brought their paralysed friend. Notice first that Jesus perceived their faith.

When the man's friends realized that they could not get through, they were determined still to reach Him; so they went up to the housetop. Luke tells us that they "let him down through the tiling with his couch into the midst before Jesus" (5:19). If only we today, who claim to know the power of Christ in our lives, were willing to be so imaginative and determined to bring to Jesus our friends in spiritual need! They did not stay to wonder who might pay for the broken roof! But we allow all sorts of things to deter us. Why? Because we are not so sure as these men were, that *here* is the help that can make all the difference.

Matthew, Mark and Luke all stress the fact that Jesus saw that these four men believed that He could help their friend. "Jesus, seeing their faith . . ." Many times Christ met people's needs because their friends besought Him to—witness the healing of the centurion's servant and the raising of Jairus's daughter. There were things that the crowd could see; their love and earnestness and perseverance; but Christ looked deeper and saw the reason for all these qualities in their faith. It was because they believed that He could and would do something to relieve, that they made their great effort on behalf of their sick friend. They were not concerned about the cost to themselves of the effort, or the rebuke that it might earn them; they did not care what other people thought. There was urgency about their action and a strong conviction that it was the right thing to do under the circumstances. How much are we prepared to put ourselves out for the needs of others?

The quality of our faith can be discerned in the answer to that question. No true Christian could ever say about any other human being, "Blow you, Joe, I'm all right". Jesus perceived the faith of these men, and He welcomed it.

Jesus perceived the need of the palsied man. We have said that Jesus could see more than the crowd around, and more than the four friends could see. They could see what was obvious. The man was paralyzed and his body needed healing. There was no doubt about that. But there was a far deeper need, indicated by Christ's statement, "Son, be of good cheer; *thy sins be forgiven thee*". Thus our Lord deals with us all; He gives before we ask, and better than we ask. This poor man has not asked for anything, but Jesus perceived his deeper need. He knew also, more surely than his four friends could discern, the true need of the ailing man, as well as the need that all could see. Evidently he was burdened by a weight more intolerable than that of his bodily pains and sickness. There are cases where the forgiveness of sin follows the outward healing: remember the thankful Samaritan cured of his leprosy! but here the remission of sin comes first. His misery came more from his sense of guilt, his accusing conscience, his unresolved fear, or some unconfessed sin. His physical disability was in some way connected with his spiritual need. His sadness came not only from bodily limitation; many people have learned to bear such things cheerfully. His misery sprang from his sin. Jesus perceived his deepest need and said, as the New English Bible puts it, 'Take heart, my son, your sins are forgiven". Many need forgiveness even more than healing.

Jesus perceived the Pharisees' thought. "But there were certain of the scribes sitting there, and reasoning in their hearts, 'Why doth this man thus speak? He blasphemeth: who can forgive sins, but one, even God?'" (Mark 2:6,7. R.V.) However, these critics were not so unreasonable as are some modern critics, who profess to receive Christianity and yet exclude the supernatural from the work of the Person of Jesus Christ. If He was merely man the Pharisees were justified. Was He wrongly grasping at a divine prerogative for Himself? Yet there was not only the evidence of the miracles at Capernaum which might have convinced them, but also the fact that, without them saying a word, Jesus had perceived how they were inwardly questioning. It was for this reason that He said to them, "What reason ye in your hearts?" Or, as Matthew puts it (9:4), "Wherefore think ye evil in your hearts?" We may begin by scrutinizing Christ, but it is not long before He is scrutinizing us. We may begin by criticizing the Bible but before long it is criticizing us. We may presume to judge God, but the final judgments are His.

Professor C. S. Lewis said, "I'm trying to prevent anyone from saying the really silly thing that people often say about Christ. 'I'm ready to accept Jesus as a great moral teacher, but I don't accept His claim to be God'. That's the one thing we mustn't say. A man who was merely a man and said the sort of things Jesus said wouldn't be a great moral teacher ... You must make your choice. Either this man was, and is, the Son of God, or else a mad man or something worse. You can shut Him up as a fool, you can spit at Him and kill Him as a demon; or you can fall at His feet and call Him Lord and God. But don't let us come with any patronizing nonsense about His being a great human teacher".

The Pharisees would have been prepared to acknowledge that He was a great teacher. One of them, named Nicodemus, did come to Him and said, "We know that thou art a teacher come from God; for no man can do these miracles that you doest, except God be with him." Jesus said to him, "You must be born again, from above, of the Holy Spirit". Nicodemus, however, was earnestly looking for the truth; these men were not. "This man blasphemeth", they said. Jesus replied,

43

"Whether it is easier to say, 'Thy sins be forgiven thee', or to say, 'Arise, take up thy bed and walk'?"

Of course, anyone could say, "thy sins be forgiven thee". It is only when the true Saviour of men comes that He can say "Rise, take up they bed and walk", something which no one else would dare to say, even though this thing is less marvellous than the other. The claim to forgive sins could not be easily disproved, but the claim to heal a disease would be exposed as false immediately.

Jesus said, "But that ye may know that the Son of Man hath power on earth to forgive sins, (he said unto the sick of the palsy) I say unto thee, Arise, and take up thy bed, and go into thine house. And immediately he arose, took up the bed, and went forth before them all; insomuch that they were all amazed, and glorified God, saying, "We never saw it on this fashion". (Mark 2:10–12).

The totality of the bodily healing was evidence of the totality of the healing of the soul. The physical recovery was an indication of the spiritual forgiveness; the forgiveness was immediate. It was assured, it was complete and it was permanent. It showed who Jesus was. It glorified God.

The man did not have to wait for the passing of time to become stronger and stronger. His cure was immediate. Both Mark and Luke tell us this. So it is with forgiveness. We do not have to wait until we are good enough, or bad enough. We do not have to earn it by our own efforts, or pay for it with our money. It comes immediately to anyone who recognizes his need and comes to Jesus. Surely when we say the Creed, "I believe in the forgiveness of sins", we mean the forgiveness of our sins, not those of others. Of course there remains a tremendous amount for the forgiven sinner to learn about Christianity, but forgiveness is immediate.

The gospel writers put it that the man was healed so that all who stood around might "know" that the Son of Man has power to forgive sins. Whether or not they were prepared to accept the evidence we do not know. But we do know this—The man himself knew that he was forgiven. It was part of his experience. He trusted Jesus Christ. When we trust Christ to take away our sin we may have the assurance of forgiveness and the certainty of eternal life. As Billy Graham said in his book, "World Aflame", "There are three ways that I may know that I have eternal life: objectively, because God's Word says it; subjectively, because of the witness of the Spirit within, and experimentally be-cause, little by little as time goes on, I can see the experimental working of God in my life. It is slower than I would like, but it is a process. Therefore, I can say: 'I know' ".

Christ said to the healed man "arise and take up thy bed and walk". It was more for him than "pardon and peace". It was also pardon and power. This para-lytic knew he was pardoned before he was healed, for Christ had said it. But the power that enabled him to arise and walk remained with him as the abiding evi-dence that His pardon was real. So it is with all who come to Christ for pardon. The reality of forgiveness will be shown by new life, new victory over sin and temptation and new joy of living. Old sinful practices become unattractive, and even abhorrent. We move with the mind of Christ. We are free from envy and resentment because we realize that we are totally de-pendent for our forgiveness on what Christ has done for us on the Cross of Calvary and not on anything we may try to do for ourselves. St. Paul said, "By grace are ye saved through faith; and that not of yourselves: it is the gift of God; not of works, lest any man should boast" (Ephes. 2:8–9).

The healed man was told to take up his bed. Because Christ had healed him there would be no relapse back into the old restrictions. How true this is of the person today who has experienced the forgiveness of Christ. He would never want to go back to the old life with all its misery, its limitations and its defeat. He has a witness to give and he wants to glorify God through it.

All the world of today is a Capernaum, and Jesus Christ is still in our midst. He still touches the lives of a variety of people in a variety of ways. In the jungle of South America the Auca Indians arise and walk in newness of life. At Evangelistic Crusades throughout the world sophisticated twentieth century people are hearing Christ's words of pardon and are being touched by the power of Christ's saving grace.

Why not you?

Perhaps you are like that paralysed man.

You have been brought to the feet of Christ by someone else.

You have been conscious of your need for a long time.

You have an attitude of faith, even though it is not expressed in words.

You hear the voice of Jesus saying, "Thy sins be forgiven thee".

You believe His words.

Then act upon them.

"Stand up for Christ.
Have done with the old life.
Walk in newness of life.
Witness to your friends.
Glorify God."

5   PASSING THROUGH JERICHO

Excavations at present in progress at Jericho suggest that it may have been the first walled city in the world. It has a history of 7,000 years. It was the first city taken by the Israelites under Joshua when they entered the Promised Land, but it had had a long history before that. It was an important place, as the evidence of seventeen successive stages of the town walls show. In the course of time the ruins of successive towns on the same site have built up a mound at least seventy feet high. By the excavations of these ruins, level by level, the history of the site can be worked out.

If the pilgrim journeys to Jericho from Jerusalem he will first pass through Bethany, where Mary and Martha and Lazarus lived. He will also see the spot where Jesus heard of Lazarus's death. In the distance is Mount Nebo where God spoke to Moses, and the plain of Gilgal.

Jerusalem is nearly 2,600 feet above sea level: Jericho is nearly 1,000 feet below; the lowest inhabited place on earth, lying at the bottom of the deepest crack in the earth's surface. In the 23 miles between the two towns you will descend over 3,000 feet, and you will do well to keep on the road; it wanders through one of the most terrifying deserts in the world—a barren trackless wilderness where nothing grows, covered with stones and completely waterless. There is nothing out of date in the Scripture that says, "A certain man went down from Jerusalem to Jericho, and fell among thieves; which stripped him of his raiment, and wounded him, and departed, leaving him half dead" (Luke 10:30). In the famous parable Jesus mentions an inn to which the Good Samaritan took the wounded man. Half-way between Jerusalem and Jericho there was until recently an inn called the "Inn of the Good Samaritan".

Beyond that point the road still drops until, turning a corner, you see a lovely green area. Jericho lies before you, the city of palms.

In Jesus' day it was a city standing at the crossroads of many caravan routes, a reward and a haven for those who had endured the perils of the wilderness around it. There are vast orchards watered by Elisha's fountain. Bananas, oranges, melons, pomegranates, figs and dates still grow. It was in Jericho that Jesus healed blind Bartimaeus. In Jericho He met Zacchaeus the tax-collector, and told him to come down from the sycomore tree because He wanted to go to his house. The friendship of Jesus began a transformation in the life of Zacchaeus. The story touches and reminds the pilgrim that obedience to the words of Christ is for him also the only way of peace.

*　　*　　*

At the loneliest and the most serious moments of your life, have you looked at other people and wondered if they too were seeking something they could not describe, but which they knew they needed? You are not alone. All mankind is travelling with you; everyone is on the same quest. All humanity is seeking the answer to the confusion, the moral sickness and the spiritual emptiness that oppresses the world.

Certainly this was true of Zacchaeus, the rich, successful chief tax collector. In Luke, Chapter 19, we are told that "he sought to see Jesus who He was". Here was a man really seeking. In the Authorized Version he is called "a publican". That does not mean that he owned the largest "pub" on the busiest corner, with the highest tariff. "Publican" in those days meant tax collector.

Rome extorted the taxes but these fell much more heavily on the people because they were farmed out to agents in every province. These agents divided the country into districts and let them to sub-agents who, having naturally paid for them in advance, sought to recoup for themselves. Being natives of the country they used their knowledge to extract as much as possible from the people.

The Jewish publicans were universally despised, branded as plundering beasts of prey, and given vilest character—"publicans and sinners" were always spoken of in the same breath, regarded as traitors both to their country and to their God. For orthodox Jews, marriage into a family in which there was one publican was forbidden. They were excluded by the Pharisees from the synagogues and no one associated with them. No one gave them a chance to repent.

The first thing we notice about this tax gatherer is his earnest resolve. Luke 19:3, reads "He sought to see Jesus who He was".

Why should *he* seek to see Jesus? Surely he had

everything he wanted—position and power, even if it had brought execration. He was the chief of the publicans. No doubt he had schemed for years to get to the top; tricked and trodden on anyone who got in his way. So many are like that.

I remember speaking to a wedding couple, and trying to point out to them the spiritual significance of their marriage. The young fellow said, "I don't pretend to be religious. Now that I'm getting married I'll need more money, which means that I shall have to tread on more people than I did before." I looked at him and then at his fianceé and said, "And will you tread on her too?"

A few months later he came to the Rectory asking for help. The marriage was breaking up.

Zacchaeus was in a top position but he needed help.

Why should he want to see this poor carpenter of Nazareth who had no interest at all in amassing a fortune for himself?

Ah—Zacchaeus was rich, but he was beginning to see the deceitfulness of riches. His wealth had not brought him happiness. Perhaps he had already heard the words of Jesus, "How hardly shall they that have riches enter into the kingdom of God! For it is easier for a camel to go through a needle's eye" (Luke 18: 24–25).

We can believe that Zacchaeus was a hard worker, only those who work hard make a lasting success of anything. He may have found it possible to salve his conscience by keeping busy. We may try this. If we stop to think, conscience catches up with us.

Zacchaeus must have had a good brain: else he would never have attained his position. Education could give him much, but it could not satisfy his emptiness of soul. He found himself trapped in the rut of his own thinking. In his need he looked in the right place for an answer, for "he sought to see Jesus".

The record tells us that he could not see Jesus: he was a short man and the crowd was in the way. But he was determined to see Jesus and nothing was going to stop him. Since he could not see over the heads of the crowd, he was bound to do something unorthodox and quite out of keeping with his dignified position as a Government man! So he did: he *ran* to climb a tree. Dignified high government officials do not normally run, and certainly they do not climb trees! But Zacchaeus did; he wanted to see Jesus. We must not allow the opinions of others to stop us when we want to see Jesus, and perhaps they will misunderstand. But if we know that something is wrong within us, and when we want more than anything else to put things right, we are not going to let anything stop us on the way to Jesus. Are you as much in *earnest as Zacchaeus was?*

The second thing we notice about Zacchaeus is: his eager response. In verse 5 we read "when Jesus came to the place He looked up and saw him, and said unto him, "Zacchaeus, make haste, and come down".'

Zacchaeus wanted to see Jesus: nothing was more certain than that; but I doubt if Zacchaeus wanted Jesus to see him! But when Jesus came to the place He looked up into the sycomore tree and said, to the great surprise of this despised, conscience-stricken, hidden man, "Zacchaeus, make haste, and come down; for today I must abide at thy house."

We cannot hide ourselves in the crowd. Jesus calls each one of us by name. We may think that we can be lost in the crowd and we may justify ourselves in our wrong-doing by claiming a certain safety in numbers. But it is useless for us to say, "Everybody does it, and lots are much worse than I am!' Sin is sin, whether it is committed by many or by few.

Jesus' call came *suddenly* to Zacchaeus. "Make haste", he said. "Don't delay". "Don't make excuses". "Don't try to explain". We must obey Christ's word as soon as we hear it. He constantly calls men and women to Himself, and when they come to Him their only regret is that they did not come earlier.

Jesus told Zacchaeus to come down from the tree. Only thus could he have fellowship with Christ,—he must come down. If you and I want fellowship with Christ we too must come down from the tree in which we find ourselves.

Is it the tree of Good Works? Some people believe that if they help as many people as they can, and try to live a good life, God will require nothing more of them. But the Scriptures tell us clearly "By grace are ye saved through faith; ... Not of works, lest any man should boast" (Ephes. 2:8–9). If you are trusting in your good works to justify you, Christ says, "Come down".

Is it the tree of Religious Observances? How often people say "Of course, I've been attending Sunday School and Church all my life." They speak in such a way as to suggest that that is all that could be expected of anyone. But such a man must not seek to use his religion as a screen against the penetrating conviction of sin by the Holy Spirit and the call of Christ to repent. To such a person Christ says, "Come down".

Is it the tree of Pride? Christ calls each one of us from this pride of place, pride of possessions, pride of person. In almost every life there is something of this sort. It is difficult for us to recognize this—and doubly hard if we are made to face this in the presence of others, as Zacchaeus was made to.

Are we ready to say with Isaac Watts "My richest gain I count but loss, and pour contempt on all my pride"?

That is what Zacchaeus did in his eager response. "He made haste, and came down, and received Jesus joyfully".

So the third thing we notice about Zacchaeus is: his energetic re-adjustment. Jesus said, "Today I must abide at thy house." I read somewhere these words:

"If Jesus came to your house, to spend a day or two,
If He came unexpected, I wonder what you'd do?
I know you'd give your nicest room to such an honoured guest,
And all the food you'd serve Him would be the very best,
And you would keep assuring Him you're glad to have Him there,
That serving Him in your home is joy beyond compare.

But when you saw Him coming, would you meet him at the door
With arms outstretched in welcome to your Heavenly visitor?
Or would you have to change your clothes before you let Him in,
Or hide some magazines and put the Bible where they'd been;
Would you turn off the radio and hope He hadn't heard,

54

And wish you hadn't uttered that last, loud, hasty
 word?

Would you hide your worldly music and put some
 hymn books out;
Could you let Jesus walk right in, or would you rush
 about?
And I wonder, if the Saviour spent a day or two with
 you,
Would you go right on doing the things you always
 do?
Would you go right on saying the things you always
 say?
Would life for you continue as it does from day to
 day?

Would your family conversation keep up its usual
 pace?
And would you find it hard, each meal, to say a table
 grace.
Would you sing the songs you always sing, and read
 the books you read?
And let Him know the things on which your mind and
 spirit feed?
Would you take Jesus with you everywhere you'd
 planned to go?
Or maybe would you change your plans, for just a
 day or so?
Would you be glad to have Him meet your very closest
 friends?
Or hope that they would stay away until His visit
 ends?

Would you be glad to have Him stay for ever, on and
 on ..

Or would you sigh with great relief, when He at last
   had gone?
It might be interesting to know the things that you
   would do,
If Jesus came in Person, to spend some time with you."

We know, within ourselves, each one of us, just
how we would have to answer the searching questions
of that poem. That helps us to appreciate what Zacchaeus needed to do—and did. He said to the Lord:
"Half of my goods I give to the poor; and if I have
taken any thing from any man by false accusation,
I restore him fourfold."

When any man sees where he stands and turns to
Jesus in repentance and faith a transformation begins
immediately; the word of assurance comes from the
Saviour Himself as it came that day to Zacchaeus.
"This day is salvation come to this house."

The seeking sinner is met by the seeking Saviour.
Zacchaeus "sought to see Jesus who He was"; "The
Son of Man is come", said Jesus, "to seek and to save
that which was lost" (Luke 19:10).

Are you seeking Jesus? However that must be
answered, remember that always, always, *Jesus is
seeking you*.

Christ asks you to make haste and come down
from your tree (whatever that may mean in your personal circumstances), He asks you to look quickly up
to *His* tree on Calvary's hill.

In Peter's Epistle we are reminded that Jesus Christ,

His own self bare our sins in his own body on the
tree, that we, being dead to sins, should live unto
righteousness: by whose stripes ye were healed
(I Peter 2:24).

Here on the tree of Calvary, on the Cross of wood, the Son of Man took your place and mine. He took our sin upon Him and paid its full penalty so that He might make available the free gift of forgiveness and the assurance of salvation to all who receive Him. To Zacchaeus in his home he said, "Today is salvation come to this house". To the penitent thief on a cross beside His own he said, "Today thou shalt be with me in Paradise." Whatever your position as you read this, you too may know in your own life, as you begin to put your faith in Christ as Saviour, that the "Son of Man is come to seek and to save that which was lost".

6   DRINKING WITH A SAMARITAN

One of the most unforgettable characters I have ever
met was the High Priest of the small Samaritan sect—
nowadays a mere remnant of three hundred or so.
Tall, grey haired, and with penetrating eyes, he stood
holding the ancient scroll of the Pentateuch in the Synagogue at Nablus in Jordan.

His strong voice penetrated the building as he sang
an ancient Samaritan song, the strange sound of which
still rings in my ears. I walked with him and a priest
of the Arab Evangelical Church to Jacob's Well, near
Sychar. Here we met a priest of the Greek Orthodox
Church, in charge of the partly completed church situ-
ated above this holy place. When he offered me a drink
from the cool, clear water of the well, how could I
refuse, as I remembered that centuries before Jesus
Himself there said to a Samaritan woman, "Give Me
to drink".

We were a strangely mixed company; yet there were
two things in common about us all—the Samaritan
High Priest, the Greek Orthodox priest, the priest of
the Arab Evangelical Church, and myself of the Church
of England. We all believed in the God of Abraham,

Isaac and Jacob, and we were all drinking together strong black Turkish coffee.

Who are the Samaritans? The Jews have always declared them to be the descendants of the Assyrian colonists who intermarried with the remnants of the ten tribes of Israel after the invasion of Shalmanezer. This mixed race, it is said, learned a garbled version of the Hebrew religion, and have persisted in their delusions ever since. They recognize only the first five books of the Old Testament, and they believe that Mount Gerizim is the place appointed by God for sacrifice. From Jacob's Well I could clearly see this revered spot where each year the sacrifice of the Passover is still made.

The Samaritans themselves claim to be directly descended from the Israelites of the land, apart from the foreigners. They claim pure descent from the families of Ephraim, Manasseh, and Levi, who escaped and remained completely separate from the Assyrian invaders. But when the Jews returned to Jerusalem, after their captivity in Babylon, Ezra refused to accept the Samaritans' offer of help in rebuilding the Temple. Incensed by this, the Samaritans retaliated in every possible way, and set up their own Temple on the top of Mount Gerizim.

Conflict continued throughout the centuries before Christ, and it was when Jesus was a boy that things reached a climax. A number of Samaritans crept into the temple precincts in Jerusalem and left dead bodies about the sacred courts, thus producing the foulest of all ceremonial pollutions. This is why it could be said of Jesus' ministry that the Jews had no dealings with the Samaritans. That gives point to Jesus' story of the Good Samaritan. It was a Samaritan who succoured the Jew who had been robbed and left half dead by the side of the road. The victim's fellow countrymen had walked by on the other side.

But fully to understand the conversation between Jesus and the woman of Samaria, we must have in mind not only this age-long quarrel but also the specialized relationships between men and women, in His day.

A Jewish man could not speak to a Jewish woman out of doors, even if he knew her, not even if she were his mother or sister! For a Jewish man to talk to an unknown Jewish woman would be even less admissable. For a Jewish rabbi to talk to a Jewish woman he did not know was incredible. For a Jewish rabbi to speak to a Samaritan *man* was unheard of. *But for a Jewish rabbi to talk to a Samaritan woman whom he did not know* would be an outrage; and if anything could further partake of the impossible it would be the thought of a Jewish rabbi talking to a Samaritan woman of doubtful reputation. No wonder the Samaritan woman was stunned with astonishment, and said, "How is it that you, a Jew, ask drink of me, a Samaritan woman?"

The conversation which follows, as recorded in John, Chapter 4, is one of the most exciting interviews in history, and although it took place so long ago, it is still completely relevant today.

First let us consider *the presence of Christ to meet her loneliness*. The loneliness of this woman may be seen in the fact that she came at a time when it seemed almost certain that no one else would be at the well. She might well have wanted to avoid the gossiping tongues of the other women who would know all about her, and perhaps there were pangs of conscience through which she would wish to avoid the company of others.

This lonely woman was captive in the tangled web of circumstances of her own weaving. But Christ came to meet her loneliness, disillusioned and despairing as she was. Surely this was no accidental meeting! Our Lord's purpose was implicit in the Bible word, that "He must needs go through Samaria" (John 4:4). Nor did he allow artificial barriers of man's making to prevent Him reaching this soul in need. He cut through the barrier of prejudice between the Jews and the Samaritans, and spoke to this Samaritan woman. He broke through the social conventions and asked the one question which was permissible to a stranger, "Give Me a drink." But having begun the conversation He worked at the problem of this lonely woman. He brushed aside the religious bigotry which she quoted; he would not be drawn into an irrelevant discussion of places of worship, right or wrong.

There are many lonely people in the world today. Not all have the same reasons for loneliness, but the remedy is the same. It is the presence of the living Christ giving strength and companionship to those who will receive Him.

Now let us consider secondly, *the provision of Christ to satisfy her emptiness.* In verses 13 and 14 we read that Jesus said to the woman, "Whosoever drinketh of this water shall thirst again: but whosoever drinketh of the water that I shall give him shall never thirst; but the water that I shall give him shall be in him a well of water springing up into everlasting life."

There was a deep longing in the heart of the woman.

61

She was so empty—she had filled her life with un-restrained desires and undisciplined living, yet she was still unsatisfied, and thirsty for peace.

A plant is known in South America which finds a moist place and sends its roots down, and which becomes green until in a short time the place becomes dry. Then it draws itself out, and rolls itself up, and is blown along by the wind until it comes to another moist place where it repeats the same process. On and on goes the plant, stopping wherever it finds a little water, but in the end, after all its wandering it is nothing but a bundle of dry roots and leaves.

It is the same with those who drink only of this world's springs. They drink, and thirst again, and go on from spring to spring, blown by the winds of passion and desire, and at last their souls are nothing but bundles of unsatisfied appetites and burning thirsts.

Jesus said, "Whosoever drinketh of the water that I shall give him shall never thirst." Is there an emptiness in your life? Does your happiness depend on where you are, what you have, whom you know? Real satisfaction comes from within, not from outside. Jesus said, "the water that I shall give him shall be in him a well of water springing up into everlasting life".

This is a well which never runs dry, a well that is eternal. It is living; its water is always fresh, it is satisfying. Are you saying with this Samaritan woman of old, "Sir, give me this water, that I thirst not"?

Let us consider, thirdly, *the perception of Christ to probe her sinfulness.* "Go, call thy husband", he said (Verse 16). The woman answered Jesus, "I have no husband". Jesus replied, "Thou hast well said, I have no husband: for thou hast had five husbands; and he whom thou now hast is not thy husband: in that saidst thou truly."

Why should Jesus awaken such memories? Why open the cupboard door and stare at the secluded skeleton? Why lay bare the secrets of that life? It was a necessary step. The wound must be probed to the bottom and cleansed before it can be healed. There must be confession before forgiveness. So it must be with us, if we would have the living water. "Go, call thy husband", could mean for us to relinquish dishonest gains, to make up some long standing argument, to recall violent, uncharitable words, to put right things which we know are wrong.

How we wince when our Lord lovingly insists on coming into such close contact with us, as a bloodshot eye dreads the light or a broken limb evades a touch! As this woman did, we are apt to start some worn out theological controversy in the hope of putting Him off, just as the woman said, "Our fathers worshipped in this mountain; and ye say, that in Jerusalem is the place where men ought to worship" (Verse 20).

In other words, she is saying, "Don't let's talk about my wrong-doing. Let's discuss anything else". But Jesus takes up and uses her evasion, giving a revelation of God's character which has influenced worship ever since. "God is a Spirit", He said, "and they that worship him must worship him in spirit and in truth."

The woman realizes that He is not to be put off; He will make her face the moral problems of her life. This ruthless, tender lover of her soul will not let her off, and will not let her go. No more evasion. She is beaten. The Hound of Heaven has tracked her down as He will track us all down at last.

Fourthly, we see *Christ's proclamation of Himself to complete her forgiveness*. To begin with this woman saw Jesus only as a Jew. "How is it that thou, being a Jew, askest drink of me, which am a woman of Samaria?" She saw Him merely as a man. Then because of His promise to provide living water she respects Him as a good man, and says, "Sir, give me this water, that I thirst not". But when His searching words probe into her sinful life and expose her for what she is, she says, "Sir, I perceive that thou art a prophet."

A further revelation was to come. The woman says, "I know that Messias cometh, which is called Christ: when he is come he will tell us all things." And Jesus says, "I that speak unto thee am he."

What do you believe about Jesus Christ? Is He just a Jew who lived in Palestine about two thousand years ago? Is He merely a good man who went about the countryside helping people in need, like some modern lover of his kind? Is it enough to think of Him as an Isaiah, a Jeremiah, a Mohammed, or a great teacher like Buddha? Or have you realized that He is the Messiah, God's Anointed One come to bring deliverance to His people?

Only Jesus Christ the Son of God has power to say, "Thy sins be forgiven thee." Are you able to say with the woman of Samaria, "Come, see a man which told me all things that ever I did. Is not this the Christ?"

Finally, let us consider *the power of Christ to use her witness*. In the excitement of her new experience of forgiveness, and in the certainty of the revelation she has received, she leaves her water pot behind her, a symbol of the water which can never completely satisfy thirst. Then she makes her way back to those who knew her former way of life, for she has drunk of the living water, which has brought her peace and satisfaction, joy and purpose, forgiveness and victory; she wants to witness to it and share it. Her transformed life was a witness to Christ's power.

Here is one last revealing word from this chapter. Many believed on Him because of the word of the woman, and many more believed because of His own word. They said to the woman, "Now we believe not because of thy saying: for we have heard him ourselves, and know that this is indeed the Christ, the Saviour of the world."

Even more was to be revealed, and we know that that same Christ who shared our humanity as the Son of Man, shared God's Divinity as the Son of God. We may in faith see on the Cross of Calvary the full revelation of His love in dying for each one of us, and participate in the complete victory of His resurrection.

But our entry into all that Christ has done for us must be just as personal as that of the Samaritan woman. We must each drink of the water of life, and we may drink freely. The Risen Christ is still on His unceasing quest. In our efforts to compromise in our unclean desires and our sins, we are ever seeking to evade Him and to escape His demands. But we can never finally put Him off. He is destined to track us down, and although there is pain for us, when we see our guilty selves with His eyes, that moment is really the happiest moment of our lives; we have found at last the only, living water which can quench the eternal thirst of the soul.

Christ is ready for all those who will come to Him in faith. "If any man thirst," He said, "let him come unto Me and drink."

7   PILGRIMAGE TO JERUSALEM

Jerusalem, one of the world's most beloved cities, is enthroned in the hearts of men everywhere as the Holy City. It is held sacred by the three great monotheistic faiths, Judaism, Christianity and Islam. The scene of Christ's ministry, of His suffering, of His crucifixion, burial and resurrection; Jerusalem, the holiest site of Christendom, has received the homage of pilgrims down the ages. Today, old Jerusalem, cradle of Christianity, this City of God, surrounded by its beautiful crenellated stone walls, overlooking the Garden of Gethsemane and the Mount of Olives, welcomes as of old, people from the far corners of the earth. The world has many cities which are larger and some which are older; but Jerusalem is unique.

Jerusalem existed in the middle of the second millennium B.C. The Bible first mentions it under the name of Salem which had for its king, Melchisedec, a priest of the most high God, a contemporary of Abraham.

When the Israelites entered Canaan, they found Jerusalem in the hands of an indigenous Semitic tribe, the Jebusites. When David became king, his first capital was Hebron, but he soon saw the value of Jerusalem and set about its capture, and made it the centre of his kingdom. He improved its fortifications and built himself a palace. He also installed the ark of the Covenant in his new capital. Solomon carried the work of fortification further, but his great achievement was the construction of the magnificent Temple.

After Solomon's death, and the division of the kingdom, Jerusalem became the capital of Judah, the southern kingdom. As early as the fifth year of Solomon's successor Rehoboam the Temple and royal palace were plundered by Egyptian troops. Philistines and Arab marauders again plundered the palace in Jehoram's reign. In Amaziah's reign a quarrel with Jehoash, the king of the northern kingdom, resulted in the destruction of part of the city walls and further looting of the temple and palace. King Uzziah repaired the fortifications so that Ahaz was able to withstand attacks by the combined armies of Syria and Israel.

Soon after this, in 721 B.C., the Northern Kingdom fell to the Assyrians. Hezekiah of Judah also had good reason to be afraid of the mighty power of Assyria but Jerusalem escaped, mainly because a tunnel was cut under the mountains bringing water to the Pool of Siloam to improve the city's water supply. Hezekiah's tunnel still remains today and the adventurous pilgrim may paddle his way through the water for the full length of 533 metres.

However, in 587 BC Nebuchadnezzar of Babylon destroyed the city of Jerusalem and the Temple. At the end of that century, the Jews, now under Persian rule, were allowed to return to their land and city and they rebuilt the city and the Temple, but the walls remained in ruins until Nehemiah restored them in the middle of the fifth century.

Alexander the Great ended the power of the Persians at the close of the fourth century and after his death Ptolemy, one of his generals, founder of an Egyptian dynasty, entered Jerusalem and included it in his realm. In 198 BC Palestine passed into the hands of the Selucid kings. Antiochus IV entered Jerusalem, destroying its walls and plundering and desecrating the Temple. Judas Maccabeus led a Jewish revolt in 165 BC, and the Temple was rededicated. The Hasmanaean dynasty then ruled a free Jerusalem until the middle of the first century BC when Rome intervened. Roman generals forced their way into the city in 63 and 54 BC. A Parthian army plundered it in 40 BC.

Three years later Herod the Great, under Roman protection, took control of the country, ruling with a fierce hand from 37 BC to 4 AD. He repaired the damages of former years, raising many beautiful buildings throughout the land, but his most renowned work was the building of the Temple on a far grander scale. Herod was by birth an Idumean, by necessity a Roman, by marriage a Jew, by culture a Greek, and he freed his subjects of all oppressors except himself. Herod was suspicious, murderous and immoral. Such was the state of the country into which Jesus was born, in Bethlehem of Judea, towards the end of Herod's reign.

A few days after His birth His parents took him to the Temple, as St. Luke records, "To present him to the Lord." The pilgrim today may stand in the large area where the ancient Temple once stood—the place where the saintly Simeon was gladdened by the sight of the baby who fulfilled the agelong Messianic expectation of the Old Testament. Yet he foresaw the cruel things which would follow, and he said to Mary, "this child is destined to be a sign which men reject;

and you too shall be pierced to the heart. Many in Israel will stand or fall because of Him" (Luke 2:35. N.E.B.).

Surveying the Temple ruins, you recall the occasion when the twelve year old Jesus came with His parents from Nazareth for the feast of the Passover. In Jerusalem He sat in the midst of the doctors, both hearing them and asking them questions, so that all that heard him were astonished at his understanding and answers. But His parents, supposing Him to be in their company, went a day's journey.

Dominating the scene of the ancient Temple is the Dome of the Rock, built in 687–691 AD, known more commonly as the Mosque of Omar. In the very heart of the building is the sacred rock emerging from its foundation, massive, gaunt and strong in striking contrast to the splendour of its setting. It is surrounded by beautifully carved balustrades. High over the Rock is the beautiful dome in all its colour and glory, one hundred and eight feet high, and supported by an ornate cylindrical drum, which in turn is supported by twelve marble pillars and four granite piers. The diameter of the dome is seventy eight feet, the lower portion being encased in marble. Higher up, the walls are adorned with Persian and Turkish tiles. Sixteen stained glass windows decorated with gold let in a soft light which sheds a subdued glow on the Rock. This is reputed to be the place where Abraham set about the sacrifice of Isaac, his son.

Here the pilgrim will remember that when Jesus was tempted in the wilderness, the Devil took him in a vision not merely to Jerusalem, not simply to the Temple of Jerusalem but to the very pinnacle of the Temple. There he said, "If thou be the Son of God, cast thyself down from hence: for it is written He shall give His angels charge over thee, to keep thee. Jesus answered, "Thou shalt not tempt the Lord thy God." As the pilgrim surveys the scene he remembers too that Jesus withstood the temptation, and that we too may share in His victory if we trust Him.

Here in the Temple area Jesus taught the people. Here He was interrupted by the Priests and the Scribes who endeavoured to trap Him with their questions. Here the Pharisees tried to make Him declare His loyalty either to Caesar or to God. Here the Sadducees attempted to draw Him into an argument about the resurrection. Here the Scribes endeavoured to undermine His authority, and here He saw the woman who cast into the treasury the two mites which were her entire possessions. When some people admired the Temple and its adornments, He said, "As for these things which ye behold, the days will come, in the which there shall not be left one stone upon another that shall not be thrown down." (Luke 21:6). Here, too, He upset the money changers' tables and cast out those who cheated the people. This was no "Gentle Jesus, meek and mild", but the strong Son of Man demonstrating the righteousness of God.

We are not surprised when the Scriptures tell us that many plotted against Him as a result of all this. Others paid great attention to His words and deeds. So today Jesus Christ moves amongst men, testing their loyalties, and asserting His authority. As in the olden days, some violently oppose Him, but others become attentive to hear him.

Here in this ancient city, too, we recall the welcome they gave as He made His way from Bethany down the Mount of Olives on that first Palm Sunday. When He came near He beheld the city and He wept over it, saying, "If thou hadst known, even thou, at least in this thy day, the things which belong unto thy peace! but now are they hid from thine eyes" (Luke 19:42). Like his Lord, the Christian pilgrim of today is moved with compassion as he realizes the position of so many all around him who are seeking peace in the wrong way, and who therefore can never find it. Now he begins to share the sufferings of Christ.

He makes his way to the Garden of Gethsemane, where eight ancient olive trees, said by some to be about 3,000 years old, still stand. Somewhere close by, after the last Supper, Jesus came with His disciples and said. "My soul is exceeding sorrowful, even unto death." Going a little distance from them and falling on His face, He prayed, "O My Father, if it be possible, let this cup pass from me: nevertheless not as I will, but as Thou wilt" (Matt. 26:38–39).

In the agony of that moment, he prayed more earnestly still, says the Book. His sweat was as it were great drops of blood falling down to the ground. Here you begin dimly to apprehend something of what it meant to the Sinless One that He should bear the sin of the whole world, your sin, and mine. You remember, too, that it was here that Judas betrayed his Lord, and you follow the crowd of soldiers to the Lithostrotos (the "Pavement"; John 19:13).

Here we tread the very stones Jesus trod. Here He was scourged, mocked, condemned and sent to His death. On the stones of this pavement you may see rough sketches made by Roman soldiers—these include a Crown of Power and a Sword of Death, separated by a series of squares, lines and circles. This seems to be a game; the winner reached the crown and the loser fell on the sword. The treatment of our Lord at this time, so difficult to understand otherwise, might be explained by this game. Here would be an occasion for the soldiers to play with a living King and, still better, a Jewish King. Worn out by the scourge, the condemned man is pushed on to the step, and the game begins.

But the Christian pilgrim knows the significance of all this. Jesus went to His death, not because He was caught up in the circumstances of the time, not because He was considered a dangerous political figure, not even to die for a good cause, or to demonstrate the depth of God's love for us; He died to pay the price of our sin, to take our penalty upon Him, and to bear in His body our sins on the tree. As Isaiah said, "With his stripes we are healed." (Isaiah 53:5) The hymnwriter put it this way;

> "Bearing shame and scoffing rude,
> In my place condemned He stood;
> Sealed my pardon with His blood:
> Hallelujah! what a Saviour!"

Our pilgrimage leads us along the Via Dolorosa until we come to the traditional place of the Crucifixion, where now the Church of the Holy Sepulchre stands. Some people follow General Gordon's suggestions about another site, and there is something to be said for these; but we look beyond the place and the time, to the true significance of the thing that happened. On the rocky knoll called Golgotha, or Calvary, the cross was fixed and the God-Man hung for six hours, for the ransom of the world. For the Christian this is not merely an historical event; it is relevant to him now; he is remembering with awe and gratitude and wonder the dying Jesus, but he experiences the power of the living Christ.

He rejoices in the story of the empty sepulchre, for it witnesses to the fact that Christ is the Son of God, risen and alive today! When I worshipped at St. George's Cathedral in Jerusalem, we sang the hymn which included the significant words, "O let me see Thy footmarks and in them plant mine own . . . "

Once again this ancient city is torn by division. The visitor realizes this as he passes through the narrow, crowded, noisy streets, teeming with people engaged in a variety of activities. The soldiers stationed above the Damascus gate are a constant reminder of the atmosphere of fear and anger which prevails. So many things seem hardly to have changed since Jesus' day—the familiar types are there—the money changer in his corner, the shop-keepers, sitting cross-legged on top of their wares, using every word and wile to persuade the unsuspecting visitor that their goods are the cheapest. The counters are covered with fruit, vegetables, cakes, buns and confections of all sorts, inviting, except for the flies! There is a hubbub of Arab voices, the hard bargaining of the salesmen, the chatter of women and the screams of little children. The crowd, the noise and the smells—it is all there. Jesus went right into the midst of human confusion like this. He went with a practical demonstration of the love of God which led Him to Golgotha's hill, but rising victorious He appeared to those who were his within this Holy City.

A visit to the Holy Land is a never-to-be-forgotten privilege; but the presence and the power of the Risen Christ may be known and experienced by all who will make a pilgrimage in heart and mind to the Christ of

Jerusalem, whether they actually see these holy places or not. This spiritual pilgrimage must be undertaken in humbleness and faith, but in the glad confidence that Jesus, the Son of God, is waiting to lead all who will follow Him to that New Jerusalem which God has prepared for all those who believe on His name.

We may end this chapter by remembering the many significant things which Jerusalem may mean for us. This city reminds us that God revealed Himself through the Jews. The Temple sacrifices were a symbol of the "one sacrifice for all" made by Christ on the Cross of Calvary. Then Jerusalem reminds us that Christianity is an historical faith. Jesus Christ is not some idealized imaginary figure. Christianity is not a system of ethical propositions. It is founded on this fact that Jesus Christ Himself, an historic person, lived in Jerusalem, ministered to the needs of people there, died and rose again from the dead, appearing there in His risen life.

So much in Jerusalem reminds us of the compassion of God's Son. He was concerned for the real human needs of people and came amongst us and shared our earthly life. He did not remain remote, impressive above the bright blue sky! He was Immanuel, "God with us".

It was there, too, close by the city, on Calvary's hill that God's plan was completed for the salvation of all who believe on Him. God's justice, as He fulfilled His own law, was met by God's love in giving His only begotten Son for this fulfillment. Justice and love came together in the death of Christ.

There in Jerusalem Christ appeared again to His disciples, demonstrating His victory over sin, over Satan, and over death! Once the disciples were convinced of this marvellous thing, that Jesus was alive again, they went out to turn the world upside-down.

Jerusalem speaks to us of Holy Spirit power, for as the disciples waited in Jerusalem as Jesus had bidden them, the Holy Spirit came to them at Pentecost in a new and personal way. Truly had Jesus said "Ye shall receive power, after that the Holy Ghost is come upon you, and ye shall be witnesses unto me both in Jerusalem, and in all Judaea, and in Samaria, and into the uttermost part of the earth" (Acts 1:8).

From Jerusalem there may spring our certainty of Heaven, for in Revelation 21, there is a vivid description of the Heavenly Jerusalem, in figurative language:

"He carried me away in the spirit to a great and high mountain, and showed me that great city, the holy Jerusalem, descending out of heaven from God ... The city had no need of the sun, neither of the moon, to shine in it: for the glory of God did light on it, and the Lamb is the light thereof. And the nations of them which are saved shall walk in the light of it: and the kings of the earth do bring their glory and honour into it. And the gates of it shall not be shut at all by day: for there shall be no night there. And they shall bring the glory and honour of the nations into it. And there shall in no wise enter into it anything that defileth, neither whatsoever worketh abomination, or maketh a lie; but they which are written in the Lamb's Book of Life."

They which are written in the Lamb's Book of Life —that means the men and women who trust in Christ as the Lamb of God who has taken away the sin of the world. The certainty of Heaven comes only to those who are trusting in Christ as their personal Saviour, who have come to Him recognizing their need, and have asked Him to take away their sin. This Holy City, this City of God, this New Jerusalem, with its walls of salvation, has its gates wide open to welcome all who will come; for Jesus said "Him that cometh to me I will in no wise cast out" (John 6:37).

8 WASHING IN THE POOL OF SILOAM

Come with me to the ancient pool of Siloam, a place steeped in history. Beginning at the foot of the Mount of Olives we continue along the Valley of Kidron until we reach Gihon, now called the Virgin's Fountain. Descend the thirty-two steps, to be greeted by giggling Arab washer-women, who shout the one word you both understand, "Baksheesh". Originally a shaft led down to the spring from the town above, and it was through this that David's commandos entered Jerusalem (II Sam. 5:8).

Hezekiah was king in Jerusalem about 700 B.C. when the Assyrians were making ready to come down "like a wolf on the fold". Facing a siege, Hezekiah was concerned to realize that the only spring of water in these barren hills lay just outside the walls of the old city of David. By cutting a long underground tunnel the king brought the spring water into the city. He sealed up the fountain and blocked the subsidiary canals leading down into the Kidron Valley, diverting his tunnel to the Pool of Siloam within the city.

All this is in II Chron., II Kings, and in the Book of Isaiah, and the accuracy of the story was established in 1880 when two boys playing in the valley discovered the tunnel and managed to crawl through it. It covers a distance of 1777 feet. It is about six feet high and in parts only twenty inches wide. At the entrance, about fifteen feet inside, there is a Hebrew inscription cut in the script of Hezekiah's day, and now in the museum in Istanbul, reading "It was cut in the following manner ... axes, each man towards his fellow, and while there were still three cubits to cut through, the voice of one man calling to the other was heard, showing that he was deviating to the right. When the tunnel was driven through, the excavators met man to man, axe to axe, and the water flowed for twelve hundred cubits from the spring to the reservoir. The height of the rock above the heads of the excavators was one hundred cubits".

I have always regretted that when an opportunist Arab offered to take me through the tunnel, I did not go with him. But time was short—and a certain consideration for hygiene also played its part! I took the safe way up above and eventually came to the Pool of Siloam, one of the few undisputed sites at Jerusalem.

I recalled that Jesus performed there one of His best-known miracles when the man born blind received his sight. This is recorded in John 9.

The story illustrates the great word of Jesus in the previous chapter, "I am the light of the world". The analogy linking spiritual sight to the touch of Christ, the Light of the world, and obedience to His word, runs deeply throughout the whole passage in John's Gospel.

The purpose of the Gospel writer in setting down this story just here is to show by analogy how light of divine salvation as expressed in Jesus Christ overcomes the darkness of man's moral and physical evil. The story is prefaced by a discussion of evil, its power and effects. "And as Jesus passed by, he saw a man which was blind from his birth." As the disciples looked at this poor man, the problem of suffering and its connection with sin worried them. "And his disciples asked him, saying, "Master, who did sin, this man, or his parents, that he was born blind?"

Of course, our Lord did not deny that sin and suffering are connected in a general way. In the long run, there would be no suffering if there were no sin. Suffering follows sin, but here and now the distribution of suffering is not according to the persons or proportions of the sinning. Saints suffer. Sinners suffer. Saints often suffer in this life more than sinners, but neither suffer in proportion to their sin. Jesus led His disciples a step higher, and in effect was saying to them that their task in this suffering world was not to speculate about its origin, or scrutinize its distribution, or to judge their suffering neighbours, but to help and heal them. This man is here, poor and blind, "that the works of God should be made manifest in him. I must work the works of him that sent me, while it is day ... As long as I am in the world, I am the light of the world".

John uses the facts of this story to make us realize that we are all spiritually blind and walk in darkness. We cannot help ourselves as we grope around in this earthly life. We keep on stumbling. We keep asking others for help. We do not know where we are going. "The god of this world (the devil) hath blinded the minds of them which believe not" (II Cor. 4:4). Paul describes the natural state of each one of us in Ephesians 4:18, "Having the understanding darkened, being alienated from the life of God through the ignorance that is in them, because of the blindness of their heart".

So when Jesus came this way, His eyes, full of compassion, fastened upon this blind man and when He had answered the disciples' question, He spat on the ground, and made clay of the spittle, and he anointed the eyes of the blind man with the clay, And said unto him, "Go, wash in the pool of Siloam", (which is by interpretation, Sent). He went his way therefore, and washed, and came seeing."

Simple instructions and immediate obedience. That is the way for all who would receive their spiritual sight.

The smearing of the eyes with mud seems to our modern minds a curious method of procuring sight, but it may have taken up and used certain beliefs of that day, and certainly stimulated the response of trusting obedience. In the same way, we may not be able to understand the remedy provided by Christ for our salvation by His death on the Cross; it may seem to intellectuals, like the ancient Greeks, to be foolishness, but its effectiveness can be tested only by obedience. But we may indeed receive our spiritual sight from Christ, the Light of the World.

Many ingenious interpretations of the story have been worked out over the years. Some see in the meaning of the name of the pool "Siloam", ("sent"), a picture of the Messiah, the "Sent One"—the one Fountain opened for the removal of all blindness and spiritual impurity. Some find in the clay a reference to the futile religious methods of the Pharisees—blind guides aggravating the blindness of men and in the washing, the mission of Jesus to wash away artificial obstructions and restore the power which these obscured.

We do not need to complicate the story with details of this sort. What we need is to follow the simple instructions by which each one may receive spiritual sight. When our attitude to Jesus is summed up in repentance for sin, faith in what Christ can do, and obedience to His Word, our eyes will be opened to a new world of God's grace and glory.

"The neighbours therefore, and they which before had seen him that he was blind, said, 'Is not this he that sat and begged?' Some said, 'This is he': others said, 'He is like him': but he said, 'I am he'."

With dramatic vividness and simplicity the narrative portrays the impression made upon those who were used to seeing a blind beggar by the wayside. At first they doubted if it could be the same person, the change was so radical.

When Christ's light streams into a man's life today, people are often amazed. Shortly after his conversion such a man told me, "You know, the people I work with just can't believe that I'm the man they knew before, and some who've just joined the firm won't believe that I used to be quite different from what I am now". When Christ comes into our lives the difference will be obvious and it will not be very long before people ask questions, just as his did when they saw the man who had been blind.

"How were thine eyes opened?" (verse 10). Of course, this man did not know much about Jesus. He had only just met Him, but the experience of His power was sufficient for him to give a faithful word of testimony. He told what he knew. He answered and said, "A man that is called Jesus made clay, and anointed mine eyes, and said unto me, 'Go to the pool of Siloam, and wash': and I went and washed, and I received sight".

You don't have to wait to witness for Jesus until you have an understanding of all the theological questions. You don't have to wait until you think you are good enough. It's not yourself you talk about. Speak about Jesus. If someone says, "But you're *different*", tell him what has happened to you. This could lead your neighbours to Christ.

"They brought to the Pharisees him that aforetime was blind. And it was the sabbath day when Jesus made the clay, and opened his eyes."

Once more the healed man speaks: he tells the Pharisees exactly what happened. They were faced with a dilemma—they must either deny the fact of the cure, or they must admit that Jesus did no wrong in making the clay and commanding a washing on the Sabbath. Some said, "No work of healing could have been done by a man who works on the Sabbath, and leads others to". But others said, "The facts are there; how can we deny them?" "And there was a division amongst them" (verse 16).

So today, when a faithful witness is given to the work of Christ in the life of a believer, some will admit it and others deny. Some are softened like wax in the warmth of Christ's love and light; others are hardened like clay.

Sadly enough, we must not be surprised if some apparently religious people reject the evidence of new life. Religion is natural to all, but while for some it becomes the avenue to spiritual reality, others use it as a means by which they avoid the facing of the truth. I recall a young man gloriously converted from a background of nominal Christianity, whose aunt immediately reacted against him when he told her of his new life in Christ, and said, "Don't talk to *me*. I've been going to church for thirty years; you've only just started". The reaction of those Pharisees is shared by many church people today, when a saved man or woman gives a vital testimony and seeks to share the experience.

* * *

"But the Jews did not believe concerning him, that he had been blind, and received his sight, until they called the parents of him that had received his sight. And they asked them, saying, 'Is this your son, who ye say was born blind? How then doth he now see?' His parents answered them and said 'We know that this is our son, and that he was born blind'."

The Pharisees, stirred up by the occurrence, summoned the man's parents. Of course, they did not deny that the man was their son, or that he had been born blind. Nor did they deny that he could now see; the miracle was obvious. But they could say nothing as to *how* he saw, and as to what had occurred. They simply said, "He is of age; ask him".

So often today we find parents who lack interest in the Christian beliefs of their children. They may admit some difference in them, but they will not admit that it was Christ Who caused it. I know of many young people who have to pursue their Christian life altogether apart from their parents.

* * *

Then the Pharisees recalled this man, so wonderfully healed, and blustered and tried to browbeat him, but he simply said, "One thing I know, that, whereas once I was blind, now I see". All attempts to persuade him to alter his story were futile. Whatever the opposition, he was standing by the facts. It is no surprise, therefore, that he was cast out. But when he had been excommunicated, Jesus came to him in his need and revealed Himself to him even more fully. This is just like Jesus, Who never leaves us alone to suffer on His behalf. Always He comes alongside us. He said to the man "Dost thou believe on the Son of God? ... It is he that talkest with thee". The inspiration of that wonderful moment was expressed in those heartfelt words, "Lord, I believe".

Here is a wonderful pattern of personal testimony. It was concise, factual and straight to the point. It was courageous, spontaneous and immediate. It was challenging, consistent and full of conviction. It was Christ-glorifying.

The testimony was first of all to new light physically received from the touch of Christ's hand, but it went on to become a testimony to a new life received by the personal revelation of Christ, the Son of God.

When we are ready Christ will reveal Himself to us in the same way, and we shall have a personal testimony to give, and a burning desire to give it.

9   LEST I FORGET GETHSEMANE

There was one place above all others in Jerusalem which I wanted to visit. It was the Garden of Gethsemane, rather less than a mile from the city. I was particularly anxious to make the pilgrimage alone, so I made my way through the city walls, with a rather inadequate guide book. First I asked directions from an Arab woman who could speak no English, but her confident gesticulations inspired me to follow her advice; but after a while I realized that I was on the wrong road, and endeavoured to cut across country. Everything was quiet except for the faint murmur from the crowded city below me, the details of which were clearly visible.

I saw in the distance two Jordanian soldiers approaching. They were young and apparently friendly; they shook me by the hand in Arab style, and at the same time addressed me in Arabic. I recognized a word or two and duly presented my passport. That did not satisfy them, and they led me to their headquarters a short way off. Pointing to the tangled barbed wire on the top of the hill they said, "Israeli—shot", "no man's land". My passport was examined in turn by three others. I endeavoured to explain that I was staying at

St. George's Cathedral, and waited for another half-hour, during which time I had visions of the inside of a Jordanian prison and a rectorless church at home! Finally I was escorted away from the demilitarized area to a track leading back to the place where I was staying: as we parted we shook hands with each other, smiled and waved goodbye.

I tried again next day to reach Gethsemane, but this time in a taxi with several others. Leaving the Jericho Road near the Palestine Museum we climbed the Mount of Olives by a new road. The old road passes the War Cemetery (1914–18) and the Hebrew University, at that time in a sort of "no man's land" between the two armies. Reaching the summit, we saw the whole city of Jerusalem below us on one side, and on the other side the Desert of Judah, with the Dead Sea at the foot of the Mountains of Moab.

The Valley of Kidron begins at the foot of Mount Scopus, to the northwest of Jerusalem, whence it slopes down, separating the city from the Mount of Olives. On this famous Mount are the Church of the Pater Noster, (where on the cloister walls the Lord's Prayer is written in forty-four languages), the Chapel of the Ascension and the multi-spired Russian Church of St. Mary Magdalene. At the foot of the mountain lies the Garden of Gethsemane, a tiny grove of ancient olive trees, surrounded by beds of flowers carefully tended by Franciscan monks. Nearby is the Basilica of the Agony which marks what is believed the spot where Jesus prayed His agonizing prayer (Luke 22:44). "And being in an agony He prayed more earnestly: and His sweat was as it were great drops of blood falling down to the ground".

I left the others so that I could walk alone through

the Garden of Gethsemane. It was hallowed ground. A strange feeling of awe and wonder humbled me as I thought of my Saviour's anguish at this very spot. Gethsemane was the scene of Christ's voluntary submission to the Will of God. As Mark tells the story, Jesus said, "Abba, Father, all things are possible to Thee; remove this cup from Me; yet not what I will, but what Thou wilt" (Mark 14:36 R.S.V). The word "Abba" was used in the home circle by a very young child to his father. No one had ever used the word to God before, but in that dark hour Jesus spoke to Him as a little child speaks to the father whom he trusts.

The significance of the words, "Thy will be done" depends on the way in which they are spoken. Jesus did not use them in broken and abject surrender, as when a man is beaten to his knees by some superior force. Nor did they express in Him some weary resignation, as when someone comes to admit that further resistance is useless and thus gives in without further hope. They were not spoken in bitter resentment, as by one who has ceased to struggle but who still rebels against the situation, nor as by one who accepts what he must accept, but who shakes his fist in the face of fate.

When Jesus said, "Not My will but Thine", it was in utter love and trust. His was a voluntary submission to God's Will. As He told His disciples He could have called on legions of angels to defend Him, had He so willed (Matt. 26:53). St. John tells us that those who went to arrest Jesus were themselves so terrified that He actually had to bid them do what they had come for (John 18:4–9). No man took Jesus' life from Him; willingly He laid it down. In all this Jesus saw the fulfilment of Scripture. He said, "I was daily with you in the temple teaching, and ye took Me not: but the Scriptures must be fulfilled" (Mark 14:49). This was no sudden emergency; events were not out of control; this was the event to which all history pointed. Whatever things might look like, God was still in control, and His purposes of redemption were being worked out.

The saintly Bishop Ryle said, "We can imagine no higher degree of perfection than that which is here set before us. To take patiently whatever God sends—to like nothing but what God likes—to wish nothing but what God approves—to prefer pain if it please God to send it, to ease, if God does not think fit to bestow it; to be passive under God's hand and know no will but His; this is the highest standard at which we can aim, and of this our Lord's conduct in Gethsemane is a perfect pattern."

All this surely helps us as we say, "Thy will be done" in our Lord's Prayer. Too often we hardly stop to realize what we say, but when some dire threat or happening brings us to use the word consciously and deliberately in the face of passing circumstances, how do we speak? Is there just a passive acceptance of the inevitable, or a weary resignation to the irresistible, or a bitter resentment against the irreconcilable?

There was a Gethsemane for Hector McMillan, his wife and six sons, along with a number of other whites who were being held by the rebels under house arrest in Stanleyville in the Congo, when the rescuing paratroopers descended. It seems that one or two rebels burst into the building and ordered the occupants outside and McMillan was shot dead in the yard of the compound. The body was brought inside and his wife spoke at a simple ceremony, telling her sons, "You boys should count it a privilege to give your daddy to Jesus Christ and the work of the Gospel in the Congo". Her prayer was, "Not my will, but Thine".

Gethsemane gives meaning to the Will of God. The Cross was at one and the same time part of the purpose and will of God, and a dreadful crime at the hands of men. At Gethsemane the sin of man was met by the love of God.

Gethsemane was the place of Christ's spiritual anguish because of man's sin. The Agony in the Garden must have been bitter indeed. No man wants to die at thirty-three, least of all in the suffering of all that crucifixion involved. On the face of it Jesus was going to His death with so little done and so much to do. His few supporters were fickle and uncomprehending. Peter, James and John slept when they should have watched and prayed; despite His warnings of the coming danger, they slept. Though they had come from the moving solemnities of the Lord's Supper, they slept. Jesus said, "My heart is ready to break with grief; stop here, and stay awake" (Mark 14:34 N.E.B.). Let this be a warning to us who claim companionship with Jesus Christ, who have walked with Him and talked with Him and declare ourselves to be His disciples. So many Christians today are asleep, insensible to the real issues of evil hovering around.

Our Lord's Word to His disciples should often ring in our ears. "Watch ye and pray, lest ye enter into temptation. The spirit truly is ready, but the flesh is weak" (Mark 14:38).

We must both watch and pray. Watching without praying may involve self-confidence and self-conceit. Praying without watching may lead to enthusiasm and fanaticism. In the Garden of Gethsemane the disciples did neither, and that contributed to the mental agony of our Lord.

But Jesus' agony was a spiritual agony as well. He "began to be sore amazed, and to be very heavy; and saith unto them, 'My soul is exceeding sorrowful unto death'." The Scriptures also tell us that "He fell on the ground and prayed that if it were possible, the hour might pass from Him".

The only reasonable explanation of these expressions is that the enormous load of human guilt began to press upon Him in a unique way. The unutterable weight of our sins was then specially laid upon Him. He was being "made a curse for us". He was being "made sin for us who Himself knew no sin". His holy nature acutely felt this hideous burden. In our Lord's agony in Gethsemane we see the exceeding sinfulness of sin. Gethsemane became the place of Jesus' spiritual anguish because of the sin of man. That is why we say repeatedly in the Litany, "By thine agony and bloody sweat, Good Lord, deliver us".

Gethsemane led to the place of Christ's substitutionary atonement for the salvation of the believer. No sooner had Jesus come to His great decision than the quietness of the garden was broken by the sound of tramping feet, the clank of arms and the shouting of men. So the drama unfolded. First there was the traitor's kiss. Matthew and Mark use the Greek word $\kappa\alpha\tau\epsilon\phi\iota\lambda\eta\sigma\epsilon\nu$ which means not only "to kiss" but "to kiss repeatedly, again and again" as a lover might. There followed Peter's desperate gesture, by which he showed himself willing to risk his life in Jesus' defence. Finally there came the arrest and the Cross.

There He was put to death in our place: as our substitute. The substitutionary theory of the Cross is not just one of a number of interpretations which may be accepted or rejected at will. For the Scriptures it is the very heart of the Atonement. The Great Shepherd of the sheep took the place of the sheep. As Isaiah wrote, "All we like sheep have gone astray … he is brought as a lamb to the slaughter". "he bare the sin of many" (Isaiah 53:6, 7, 12). When Paul spoke of "The Son of God, who loved me and gave himself for me" (Galatians 2:20) he put the fact of Christ's death at Calvary in personal terms that are as true today as in the first century.

A saintly African Christian once told a congregation that, as he was climbing the hill to the meeting, he heard steps behind him. He turned and saw a man carrying a very heavy load up the hill on his back. He was full of sympathy for him and spoke to him. Then he noticed that His hands were scarred and he realized that it was Jesus. He said to Him, "Lord, are you carrying the world's sin up the hill?" "No, My son" said the Lord Jesus, "not the world's sin; your sin!"

Christ did indeed die for for the sins of the whole world. "The Lord hath laid upon Him the iniquity of us all" (Israel 53:6). But for each one of us the important question is, "Do I realize that He has taken the load of my sin? Have I recognized Him as my personal Saviour? Have I surrendered my will to Him? Have said, 'Not my will, but Thine'?"

"Lest I forget Gethsemane,
Lest I forget Thine agony,
Lest I forget Thy Love for me,
    Lead me to Calvary."

10   THE PLACE CALLED CALVARY

"And when they were come to the place, which is called Calvary, [the place of a skull] there they crucified him, and the malefactors, one on the right hand, and the other on the left" (Luke 23:33).

Some people have little or no sense of direction, and I am one. But perhaps I could be excused for losing myself in the old walled city of Jerusalem, with its narrow, winding, crowded lanes. Standing by one of the many street stalls with their great variety of fruit, vegetables and impossible looking confections, was an Arab lad with an eager eye for business. I said to him in simple English, "Which is the way to the Damascus Gate?" "Come with me", he said, "I'll show you". A second lad came up beside me, and whispered, "Don't go with him. He will want money. I'll show you". However, I felt obliged to follow the first lad and determined that I was not going to be "taken in". The other lad came too.

We made our way through the crowded streets. The noise was almost overpowering with the chatter of women, the screams of little children, the bargaining of men, the laughing, the crying, the coughing, and the spitting. I remembered that it was through lanes like this that the Son of Man walked; it was to people like these that He talked.

In time we reached the Gate. Above, on the walls hidden between sandbags, were Jordanian soldiers with their rifles poised ready for any emergency. The hatred which exists between the Arabs and Jews must be as great as that which existed previously between the Jews and the Samaritans.

I paid the lad what I thought was a reasonable fee. He looked at the coins and then at me. Then, with a rapid flow of English such as I've never heard, he said repeatedly, "not enough, not enough, not enough". I gave him a little more, but still he protested, "not enough".

Eventually, I was rescued by the second lad who assured me that I had given quite sufficient. When the argument was over the second lad said, "Where do you want to go from here? I will show you. I do not want any money". I said, "I want to go to the Church of the Holy Sepulchre". "Follow me", he said. As we walked together he told me that he had been brought up in a Christian hostel and that he was himself a Christian. It was a welcome change to find someone whom I felt I could trust. So we came to the Basilica of the Holy Sepulchre. This sacred building is in a deplorable state, which offends the aesthetic sense of every Christian pilgrim. Attempts are now being made to improve the situation, but progress is slow, because the rights and interests of so many separate denominations demand recognition, and it is very hard to get them to work together. The Turkish Government had been selling it piece-meal over the centuries and today

BATCH CONTROL SLIP
COUNTERFOIL

CROSSED WARRANTS

*ORDINARY
*CONTINUATION BOOK
*TO CLOSE ACCOUNT
*LEAVING ZERO BALANCE

*Delete inapplicable

E

THIS IS

A

PUNCHING D

SB 597A (Counterfoil)
SBZ 597A (Counterfoil)

many claims exist. There is but one entrance, and this is in the keeping af the Nusaibeh family of Jerusalem Moslems. Three major denominations, the Roman Catholic, the Greek Orthodox and the Armenian, have the main control of the building, but three minor communities also have rights—the Copt, the Syrian Orthodox and the Abyssinian.

My new-found friend said he would wait for me outside so that I could be sure of finding my way back. I thanked him and walked into the place marked out from earliest times as the scene of our Lord's crucifixion, and of His sepulchre, from which He arose gloriously on the third day. The atmosphere was overpowering. There were people jostling from one shrine to another; numerous candles, providing a feeble illumination, one of which was thrust into my hand; processions of pilgrims led by chanting priests; monks, nuns and tourists making their acts of devotion before the numerous altars in ornately decorated chapels, and the smell of incense wafting through the crowd of curious sightseers. The Greek chapel is covered with paintings and hung with many lamps. The altar stands on the rock which, it is claimed, bore the Cross. Beneath the altar is a disc covering the place where the Cross was fixed. Putting down your hand in the centre you may touch the rock itself. I asked myself, "Was this the place where Jesus died?" With that question still in my mind, I made my way outside and there waiting for me was my friend.

When we reached the Damascus Gate again I felt that although he had disclaimed any desire for payment, it was only fair that I should pay him something, and said, "I hope you don't mind, but would you accept this?", to which he replied as quick as a flash, "not enough, not enough, not enough"!

* * *

In Jerusalem there is another possible site of the Crucifixion—a green hill outside the present city wall, shaped like a human skull. General Gordon used to meditate and pray nearby; a beautiful garden has now been made there. An ancient tomb has been discovered there and many think that this may have been the actual place where Jesus' body was laid. I stood in that garden and looked up to the green knoll behind it, shaped like a skull, with two great holes for eyes. Luke's words which head this chapter came to mind. I could visualize three crosses on that hill.

Matthew and Mark describe the two malefactors as thieves. They were not robbers in the sense of being petty criminals or sneak-thieves, but the word used means "brigands". Doubtless they were reckless adventurers and outlaws and men of courage. By the laws of the time they deserved to die.

When the three condemned men reached the place of crucifixion, each cross was laid flat on the ground. The victim was then laid upon it. As the victim was stretched upon the cross, the nails were driven through his hands. Half way up the upright beam of the cross there was a projecting ledge of wood, called the saddle, on which part of the weight of the condemned man's body rested; otherwise its weight would have torn the nails clean through his hands.

Prisoners often cursed and swore in the agony of that moment and shrieked and spat at their executioners Jesus prayed, "Father, forgive them: for they know not what they do". Then in a moment of searing agony the cross was lifted up and set in its socket with the victim hanging on it.

There is a sense in which we all may be thieves. To steal is to rob a person of something which belongs to him, or to deprive him of his due. The theft of money is not the only infringement of the commandment, "Thou shalt not steal". Tax evasion is robbery, and so is defrauding the customs. A man who does not really work the hours he is paid for is a thief. The world may say, "Finding's keeping", but God calls it stealing. What man calls scrounging, God calls stealing. To overwork and underpay one's staff is to break the eighth Commandment. Few are scrupulously honest in personal and business affairs. The commandment says flatly, "Thou shalt not steal". What does that mean to us? Here is Martin Luther's answer: "We are to fear and love God so that we do not take our neighbour's money or property, or get them in any dishonest way, but help him to improve and protect his property and means of making a living".

It's possible to steal a person's reputation. Do you repeat what other people have said—particularly unjust criticism, unconfirmed stories, unkind gossip? Then you are as guilty of stealing as the impenitent thief on the cross.

Perhaps your sin is not stealing. It may be one of the other nine commandments in which you offend.

"You shall have no other gods before me". God's demand for man's exclusive worship. It is not necessary to worship the sun, the moon, the stars, to break this law. We break it whenever we give to something or someone else the first place in our thoughts or our affections—sport, hobbies, friendship, pleasure, study.

"You shall not make any graven image". The first Commandment concerns the object of our worship, the second the manner. We may never have made some graven metal image with our hands, but what about the image of our mind? We may go to church, but do we ever really worship God? We may say prayers, but do we pray? We may have a Bible, but do we read it?

"You shall not take the name of the Lord your God in vain'. To call God "Lord" is to take His name in vain, if we do not do what He commands.

"Remember the Sabbath day, to keep it holy". The Sabbath is not our day to do with as we like, but the Lord's Day, worship of Him and service to Him.

"Honour your father and your mother". It is too easy to be ungrateful and neglectful and to fail to show to our parents the respect they deserve.

"Thou shalt not kill". If looks could kill, many would be dead. "Whosoever hateth his brother is a murderer" (I John 3:15).

"You shall not commit adultery". This commandment condemns all those relaxations of strict morality which it is so easy to gloss over. It includes having a "honeymoon" while still only engaged, indiscriminate flirting, "adventure" and experimenting. It includes all solitary sexual experience. It includes the reading of suggestive literature. Just as to entertain murderous thoughts in the heart is to commit murder, so to entertain adulterous thoughts in the heart is to commit adultery (Matthew 5:28).

"You shall not bear false witness"—a term which covers the telling of lies, misrepresentation, deliberate exaggeration.

"You shall not covet". Covetousness belongs to the

98

inner life, lurking in the heart and mind. Civil law is not concerned with coveting unless it breaks out in some act of theft. But the desire to possess the house, or goods or wife of another may foster within, and will always spoil and pervert a life.

The Ten Commandments are based deep in the Will of God, and are of an awful force and power. When C. H. Spurgeon, later called the prince of preachers, was fourteen, a conviction of sin which had begun when he was only ten, rushed in full flood over him. "I do not hesitate to say that those who examined my life would not have seen any extraordinary sin, yet as I looked upon myself I saw outrageous sin against God. I was not like other boys; untruthful, dishonest, swearing and so on. But of a sudden, I met Moses carrying the law ... God's Ten Words ... and as I read them, they all seemed to join in condemning me in the sight of the thrice holy Jehovah".

God forbid that we should remain ourselves in the place of the impenitent thief, "dead in trespasses and sins". For him as for us all, there stood open the door to repentance and forgiveness, but he died in sin.

On Calvary's central cross hung Jesus Christ, the Son of God. This cross reveals God in action against our sin. Here we see His everlasting work of *redemption*. This word denoted the buying of a prisoner of war from captivity, or the emancipation of a slave by the payment of a price. Christ is our Redeemer because He paid the price of redemption and has freed the sinner from the bondage of sin. Another word for what God has done is *reconciliation*. Man has been alienated from God by his wrong-doing, and enmity can be removed only when the root of the trouble has been dealt with. This Christ did by taking away sin and so bringing reconciliation. From another aspect we may call His work *propitiation*—the turning away of God's wrath against us. God is utterly hostile to sin, but Christ has suffered the full measure of His wrath. The word *justification* is used to indicate the position of the man who trusts in Christ's death. He is justified before God, not through anything he has done, but simply because Christ has made the way open, Himself paying the penalty of our sins.

"While we were yet sinners, Christ died for us". It is easy enough to love those who love us; anyone can do that. It is less easy to love those who differ from us. It is much harder to love those who hate us; only God's power can make it possible. "But God commendeth his love toward us, in that, while we were yet sinners, Christ died for us" (Romans 5:8).

God met the full price of our sin Himself; this shows the marvel of His love's extent.

*   *   *

There was another cross on Calvary.

Luke tells us that one of the thieves was drawn to Jesus even on his Cross. He rebuked his fellow brigand, reminding him that they deserved their fate, while Jesus was guiltless. Then he made one of the most amazing appeals in all history. To a broken Galilaean hanging in agony on a cross, mocked by the political leaders, the religious hierarchy, the army personnel, the university staff, the big business men and the rabble in the crowd, this thief said, "Lord remember me when thou comest into thy Kingdom" (Luke 23: 42). Here was a death-bed repentance. *It is never too late*. No one need ever think, however old or sick he is, however much he may have turned from God in the past, that it is too late to come to Him in repentance. How gracious is our loving Heavenly Father!

Studdert Kennedy, known affectionately during World War I as "Woodbine Willie," reminds us of this in his poem, "Today Thou shalt be with me".

> "I remember a day,
>   When they blazed away,
> And they bust up a church to bits:
>   But the cross still stood,
>   It were only wood.
> This pain—it's givin' me fits.
>
>   Ay, there it stands,
>   With its outstretched hands,
> And I can't help wonderin' why.
>   I can't quite see,
>   Is 'E lookin' at me?
> O Gawd, am I goin' to die!
>
>   I can't! Not yet!
>   My Gawd, I sweat!
> There's a mist comin' over my eyes.
>   Christ, let me be,
>   Today, with Thee.
> You took a *thief* to Paradise!"

It's never too early, either! Why wait until you are old, or sick or dying? Christ came to make life more abundant. No one is too young to experience the forgiveness and victory which Christ offers. Here is a special call to the young, in the full zest of life with all its potentialities, its vigour and its vision.

You will never by yourself be so good that you do not need Christ's reconciling work. "All have sinned, and come short of the glory of God" (Romans 3:23). All men need God's forgiveness.

You are never too bad. No one need say, "I have gone too far. I have sinned so badly that there is no forgiveness for me". The invitation of Christ is for all who will come. "Him that cometh to me I will in no wise cast out". What could be plainer than that?

Christ's promise is as certain for every man—any man—as it was for the penitent thief. "Today thou shalt be with Me".

11 BREAKFAST ON THE SEA OF GALILEE

It was the Sabbath when I reached Tiberias, on the shores of the Sea of Galilee. Streets were deserted, shops were closed, and no taxis were available; so I walked a good half-mile up-hill, carrying my heavy cases to the Hospice where I was to stay.

My room overlooked the famous Sea. The water was ruffled only by a slight wind. It was not uniform in colour; there were patches of dark and light blue, and touches of pale green. I could hardly wait to make my way to the shore. The broad outline of the landscape has not changed since Jesus walked and talked with people here. The hills are the hills he looked upon; the water makes the same splashing sound.

It is an indescribable spiritual experience to look first on Galilee. The very word "Galilee", which means "circle" is like soft music. The hymn-writer's words came immediately to my mind:

> "O Sabbath rest by Galilee!
>   O calm of hills above,
> Where Jesus knelt to share with Thee
> The silence of eternity,
>   Interpreted by love!"

But this small sea is subject to sudden storms. It is pear-shaped, only twelve to fourteen miles long, and seven miles across at the broadest point. It lies seven hundred feet below the level of the Mediterranean. It is this great depth, together with the gullies which funnel the wind into it from the east, which makes it so subject to sudden storms. The cold currents from the snowy Hermon rush down to displace the heated air rising over the sea. Waves rise as high as thirty feet, and spray may be felt two hundred yards from the shore.

My first night's sleep at Tiberias was disturbed by the roaring of the waves and the noise of the wind. It was during such a storm that Jesus showed His power over the forces of nature, and His concern to calm the frightened disciples, when He said, "Peace, be still".

Tiberias today is the capital of Galilee, the hub of its communications and the centre of an extensive agricultural hinterland. The old part has eight thousand inhabitants; the new part, twelve thousand. Hot mineral springs flow in the vicinity. Tiberias is about two thousand years old. In 20 A.D. Herod Antipas began to build here on the ruins of an ancient town. He named the new city, "Tiberias", in honour of the Emperor Tiberius. After the destruction of Jerusalem in 70 A.D., Tiberias and Galilee superseded Judah; the seat of the great academy of rabbinic learning was here. Here lived famous sages. Here the Mishna was completed in about 200 A.D., and the Jerusalem Talmud about 400 A.D. Here, too, the vowel and punctuated Hebrew script was originated.

Under Arab dominion, Tiberias became an important centre. In 985 A.D. an Arab geographer mockingly described the life of the population. He said, "For two months they gorge themselves upon the fruits of the jujube bush, which grows wild and cost them nought. For two months they struggle with the numerous flies that are rife there. For two months they go about naked because of the fierce heat. For two months they play the flute, for they suck sugar cane which resembles the flute. For two months they wallow in mud, for the rain makes their streets muddy; and for two months they dance in their beds because of the legion of fleas with which they are infested". It was said that the king of fleas holds court at Tiberias.

On the Saturday night I attended a Hebrew Christian church service. It drew together the handful of Israeli Christians who sang very movingly in Hebrew, the well-known hymn,

"Jesus shall reign where'er the sun
Doth his successive journeys run;
His kingdom stretch from shore to shore,
Till moons shall wax and wane no more".

In Jesus' day the lakeside was a busy industrial area, with at least ten towns or more along the coast, each with at least fifteen thousand inhabitants. It is estimated that there were two hundred and five cities, towns and villages in the Galilee area. It was in the filthy streets of such sordid little towns that the Son of God walked. As you make your way along the shore you may see fishing boats and nets and fishermen— you could be standing on the very spot where Jesus stood after His resurrection, when He made Himself known to some of His disciples.

John recorded the happening in the 21st Chapter of his Gospel. "After these things Jesus shewed himself

105

again to the disciples at the sea of Tiberias; and on this wise shewed he Himself" (v. 1).

His presence brought relief from restlessness to these disciples. The last week in Jerusalem had been a trying and confusing period in their lives. Jesus had compressed much teaching into a few days. He shattered for them their hopes of an outward kingdom, and one of their number betrayed him to the priests. All forsook Him when He went to the Cross, and then they hunted them as partisans of a discredited impostor. Then came the marvel of the Resurrection, and His appearances.

It is not surprising that they withdrew to Galilee, a great distance away from Jerusalem, a city strange to them, where unnerving events had followed with dizzy rapidity. Galilee was the same as ever; the familiar haunts, the sight of fishing boats rocking gently on the Lake, the smell of the fish, and then their desire to be busy again.

"Simon Peter saith unto them, 'I go a fishing'." Here we see that driving initiative, so characteristic of Peter. It must have been a very difficult time for the disciples, not knowing when Jesus might show Himself again. Peter attempts to deal with his restlessness, and says, "I go a fishing". He reacted in a similar way in the Garden of Gethsemane, when at the tense moment when the armed band arrived to take Jesus away, Peter drew his sword and swung at Malchus, the servant of the High Priest.

When Peter said, "I'm going fishing", the others said "We also go with thee". But it brought no relief for their restlessness; indeed things seemed even worse, for "that night they caught nothing". The demonstrative pronoun is used: "that *particular* night"; a night which stood out in their memory. How often in our experience we seek relief for our restlessness through action, when we ought to wait for the word of the Lord! How often we rely on our own initiative and our own resources in Christian service, instead of waiting for Christ's direction in complete dependence upon Him. We catch nothing. Our hard, long labour is wasted.

"When the morning was now come, Jesus stood on the shore; but the disciples knew not that it was Jesus" (v. 4). Commentators have pointed out the significant contrast in the position of the Lord to that of the disciples; Christ on the firm ground, the disciples on the restless waters. It is difficult to explain the failure of the disciples to recognize Christ. It can hardly have been that they were too far from the shore; they were only about 100 yards away. The failure of the two disciples at Emmaus to identify Him at first, and the failure of Mary Magdalene to recognize Him when she first saw Him, may indicate that the Risen Christ was not recognizable unless He chose to manifest Himself.

"Then Jesus saith unto them, 'Children, have ye any meat?' They answered him, 'No'."

The word used is a word of affectionate address, such as "friends". The question is asked with the use of a negative form which anticipates a negative answer. "You haven't anything to eat, have you?" He did not mean, "Have you something for Me to eat?", or "I would like to buy some fish", but He intended to rivet their attention on the fact that their return to their former occupation had been a complete failure. They had failed to reckon sufficiently with God's plan for their lives. It is as if He were saying, "You have caught nothing at all now, have you? Without Me you can do nothing. Now I will show you where to cast your net in order to catch fish".

"He said unto them, 'Cast the net on the right side of the ship, and ye shall find'. They cast therefore, and now they were not able to draw it for the multitude of fishes". (v. 6).

The command was unorthodox for fishing, but they were rewarded with a catch so great that they had difficulty in putting it in the boat. The Lord was there in the midst of their disappointment with the right command. Whatever is done in obedience to the Lord's command results in overwhelming success.

* * *

"Therefore that disciple whom Jesus loved saith unto Peter, 'It is the Lord'. Now when Simon Peter heard that it was the Lord, he girt his fisher's coat unto him, (for he was naked) and did cast himself into the sea" (v. 7).

Notice John's reticence. He calls himself "the disciple whom Jesus loved", and that could have been any of them. In v. 2 he calls himself "the son of Zebedee"; he does not mention his own name. In v. 8 of chapter 20 he calls himself "that other disciple". He never pushed himself forward. Notice also the perception of John. He is the one who said, "It is the Lord". Instantly John grasped what had happened. It was John who saw and believed on the Resurrection morning, seeing the position of the linen clothes in the sepulchre. John was the first to perceive, but Peter was the first to act. Here was the contemplative man and the practical man, the passive and the active, working together. In the service of God the man of vision and the man of action complement each other. John and Peter were often associated. At the Beautiful Gate of the Temple, when the man lame from birth was healed, it was Peter and John who were together. Peter and John were asked by the other apostles to go to Samaria to encourage the new believers there. People of differing temperaments may often work effectively together in the comradeship of service.

Once they had responded, "The other disciples came in a little ship; (for they were not far from land, but as it were two hundred cubits,) dragging the net with fishes. As soon then as they were come to land, they saw a fire of coals there, and fish laid thereon, and bread.

Jesus saith unto them, 'Bring of the fish which ye have now caught'. Simon Peter went up, and drew the net to land full of great fishes, an hundred and fifty and three: and for all there were so many, yet was not the net broken." (vv. 8–11).

When they arrived they found that somehow provison had already been made, but Jesus asked them to bring the newly caught fish. So Peter, like the man of action he was, got into the dinghy where it was beached, and dragged the net, now attached to its stern, to dry land. According to custom, they counted the fish—153. There seems to be no significance in the number. Such a number, however, might easily have broken the net, but it bore the heavy weight. God's gift is always more than we can receive, yet it never bursts the vessel which we can offer for its reception.

His Presence further assured them of His resurrection. "Jesus saith unto them, 'Come and dine'. And none of the disciples durst ask him, 'Who art thou?' knowing that it was the Lord. Jesus then cometh, and taketh bread, and giveth them, and fish likewise. This is now the third time that Jesus shewed himself to his disciples, after that he was risen from the dead". (vv. 12–14). No one asked the Stranger who He was, and to demand His authority for giving them orders. The authority and the reality of the Risen Christ is so reassuring that although they had questions they did not want to ask them. Is that not so with us? None of us would say that we know all the answers, but in the presence of the Risen Christ we do not need to ask questions.

Archbishop William Temple significantly suggested that the meal consisted partly of what our Lord Himself had prepared, and partly of what the disciples had brought to land. This is a true symbol. When we work with the Lord it is partly what He gives and partly what He helps us to offer. It is all His gift, and the whole fruit of our labour is His, not ours.

This was a specially significant time for Peter. The draught of fish would remind him of the day Jesus said, "Launch out into the deep", and he had answered, "At Thy word I will let down the net". When Peter had seen the great draught of fishes he said, "Depart from me; for I am a sinful man, O Lord". Jesus said to him, "Fear not; from henceforth thou shalt catch men" (Luke 5:10). So he forsook all and followed Him.

As Peter saw this great heap of fishes he would think of many former happenings. As he plunged into the water he would recall the time when Jesus walked on the sea towards him, and he asked that he might go to Him. When Jesus said, "Come", Peter did begin to walk on the water, but the boisterous waves frightened him, so that he began to sink but called out in a simple sincere prayer, "Lord, save me". Then Jesus gave him a name, "oligopiste", which means "O thou of little faith" Peter responded, "Of a truth Thou art the Son of God" (Matthew 14). Then, too, as he looked at the bread and the fish on the fire he would recall that on these very shores five thousand men, with women and children, had come together to hear his Master, and became hungry. Jesus took what a small lad offered, five barley loaves and two small fishes, and before Peter's eyes they were all fed from the hand of Christ. He would recall too what Jesus said about the Bread of Life, and how the crowd drifted away until only the twelve were left, and how Jesus said to them, "Will ye also go away?" (John 6:67). Peter would remember how he had said, "Lord, to whom shall we go? thou hast the words of eternal life".

Then as he looked into the flickering flame of that small fire, he would recall the time not very long ago, when he looked into the smouldering embers in the High Priest's courtyard. He would remember his words of denial, when three times he said, "I know not the man", and the eyes of Jesus as He turned towards him. Peter would remember how bitterly he wept because he had failed.

These were challenging circumstances for him. They made him see himself as he really was, and they forced him to cast aside all pretence. Jesus simply allowed the circumstances in which Peter was placed to speak to him. Sometimes Christ does that for us. He reminds us how we have vowed ourselves to Him and how we saw His mighty power in our very midst. He gently reminds of times of former failure.

In the story that follows Jesus seems to have taken Peter aside, and three times He asked him a question. What appears to be a confidential conversation came in the form of a threefold question. Jesus asked, "Simon, son of Jonas, lovest thou me more than these?" Notice the name used. It was "Simon, son of Jonas", not Peter, "the rock man", and not even "oligopiste", but simply, "Simon, son of Jonas", the name he bore before Christ first called him. More than what? These nets? These boats? These fish? These others? Peter had, in fact, protested a loyalty stronger than the rest by claiming earlier that although others would deny Christ he would be prepared to suffer prison and death. Jesus asked plainly, "Do you love me more than these now?" Again He said to him, "Simon, son of Jonas, lovest thou me?" and this he asked again after Peter's answer. Each time in this confidential conversation our Lord brings Peter a little lower. First it is, "Do you love me more than these?", and then simply, "Do you love me?", and thirdly, "Have you regard for me?", when a different word for "love" is used. All that Peter can reply is, "Thou knowest all things; thou knowest that I love thee".

So our Lord brings Peter to face the very facts about Himself. We are all of us in the same position. How can we pretend a love as great as our Lord requires? But the wonderful truth is that Jesus accepts the weakest love we can offer. He says to us as He said to Peter, "Feed my sheep". When we come in all humility without pretence, and knowing that the Risen Christ seeing into the deep recesses of our hearts, knows our every motive and desire, we may receive a new commission.

It is remarkable that in the midst of this fishing scene Christ should say, "Feed my sheep". This shows the Christian's dual responsibility; he who is required to be a fisher of men, bringing men and women to Christ, is at the same time to be a shepherd to those who have begun in the Christian life but need much guidance and protection.

To fulfil Christ's commission requires complete commitment on the part of each one of us. Yet so often there are things which hold us back. Are we tied still to the claims of our old nature, hindered by a sense of former failure or the guilt of past sins, or the realization of our personal weakness? Jesus wants to manifest Himself personally to each one of us, but He comes demanding complete commitment. It is most significant that at the end of His conversation with Peter, our Lord said, "Follow Me". He brought Peter back to the time, by the Sea of Galilee, when He first called him Peter when Peter's commitment had been immediate and complete.

Between these two significant occasions Christ Himself had experienced Calvary and the Resurrection. He had died upon the Cross for the sins of all the Peters in the world, and risen again to meet them in personal encounter. He says to Peter very definitely, very personally, and with full forgiveness, "Follow Me".

In spite of all our failure, He says the same to you and to me.

There is barbed wire where we stand, and a closely
guarded border line in this modern Jerusalem, which,
like the Israel of today shows amazing progress, and
the swift rising of modern buildings. Our view includes Mt. Scopus, Mt. Zion, and Old Jerusalem. Rab-
bis and bearded orthodox Jews in long black robes,
with side curls and broad flat hats, stand talking together. The number of orthodox Jews has been greatly
increased by refugees from countries which the Nazis
terrorized. They adhere rigidly to the Sabbath laws,
and recently some who walked or drove through the
orthodox quarter on the Sabbath have been stoned.

The visitor is taken to Mt. Zion and there shown
what is believed to be David's tomb, sacred to the Jews.
Close by is the Chamber of Martyrs, dedicated to the
memory of six million Jews slaughtered by the Nazis
in the Second World War. You will see Old Testament
scrolls which are there, stained with blood and ripped
by bayonets as the frightened Jews hopelessly held these
Scriptures closely to them in the synagogues for protection.

Nearby is the cenaculum or Upper Room. The present
building dates from the 14th century and there is ancient

evidence to support the claim that this is truly the place where Jesus met with His disciples. The Moslems turned the Church into a Mosque, but today the Israeli government prohibits the use of the building for worship.

The meeting of the disciples recorded in Acts 2:1 probably took place here: "And when the day of Pentecost was fully come, they were all with one accord in one place." This in obedience to Christ's command, for at the time of His Ascension, He had told them to remain at Jerusalem. (Luke 24:49). "Behold I send the promise of my Father upon you: but tarry ye in the city of Jerusalem, until ye be endued with power from on high."). In Acts I we read that one hundred and twenty disciples were gathered together. They chose Matthias to replace Judas as one of the Twelve. The following chapter speaks of a wonderful revelation of the Holy Spirit. This does not overlook the previous activity of the Holy Spirit in the world to which the Old Testament Scriptures make constant reference; but He came in a new and personal way. One of the conditions of His coming thus, was the obedience of the disciples. The power from on high came upon them because they were obedient. When Church congregations or individual Christians want that power to meet the contemporary challenges they must prepare in the same way for its reception.

We must also remember their unity; "they were *all* with *one* accord in *one* place." The words "with one accord" come repeatedly throughout Acts (1:14; 2:1, 46; 4:24; 5:12; 15:25). This does not refer to a unity of organization. These were the early days of the Christian Church, and Church order had not yet developed as it subsequently did. There are so many discussions and conferences today about unity: they often seem to envisage some mammoth organization. If we can all get together, some say, perhaps finally under the Pope as a key figure, all would be well. The world, seeing this impressive body, will begin to take notice and things will happen. But each separate Church must be a power in itself before it can contribute to some greater body.

The disciples' unity was centred in the beliefs about the person of the Lord Jesus Christ. They knew that the Babe of Bethlehem was the Ancient of Days, that the one who was pierced at Calvary was He who upheld all things by the word of His power, and that the one who had been the victim of wicked men was the triumphant victor over sin, death and the grave. They had seen Him die and rise again, declared the Son of God with power by that resurrection. They had watched Him ascend to glory, until a cloud received Him out of their sight, and they believed that He had passed within the veil into the Holy of Holies, and was seated at the right hand of God as their great High Priest, Intercessor and Advocate, the One Mediator between God and men. This is the unity in which Christians shared at Pentecost. This is the unity that Paul refers to in Ephesians 4, v. 5, when he says, "One Lord, One Faith, One Baptism." This is the oneness shared by all true believers in all the denominations today. To the extent that we are found to be *all* with *one accord*, to that extent the Spirit of God will be poured upon us in reviving power.

Obedient and of one mind—they were expectant, too. We might have expected to find them depressed when their Master left them, physically; but we read rather that after His ascension into heaven they returned to Jerusalem not with sadness, or disillusionment, or loneliness, or despair, *but with great joy.* They might well, knowing their weakness, have been depressed, and the impossibility of the task which now was theirs. They were to go out into the world, to face Rome all its authority, power and military might, to face the Greeks with all their philosophy and worldly wisdom, and to face the barbarians in their perverted forms of worship and living. They had no organization behind them, no missionary society supporting them and praying for them, no university training to prepare them; but their training had been received at the feet of Jesus. They knew that He loved them. He taught them. He saved them. He was real to them, and they trusted Him to fulfil His promise, "Ye shall receive power, after that the Holy Ghost is come upon you: and ye shall be witnesses unto me both in Jerusalem, and in all Judaea, and in Samaria, and unto the uttermost part of the earth" (Acts 1:8). They believed that the Lord would fulfil His promise, and that Joel's prophecy would be fulfilled, "And on my servants and on my handmaidens I will pour out in those days of my Spirit; and they shall prophesy:" (Acts 2:18).

They were expectant. Let us also be of one mind; let us confess our lack of power; let us take hold of God's promise in joyful expectancy that He will give us too the blessing of the fulness of the Holy Spirit as we wait in obedience.

* * *

"And suddenly there came a sound from heaven as of a rushing mighty wind, and it filled all the house where they were sitting. And there appeared unto them cloven tongues like as of fire, and it sat upon each of them. And they were all filled with the Holy Ghost, and began to speak with other tongues, as the Spirit gave them utterance." (Acts 2:2–4).

There was no mistaking this great experience. The whole company shared in it—not just some favoured few. The wind filled *all* the house; the fire sat upon *each* of them; they all used other tongues. Nor did it depend upon an appeal to one only of the five senses, but to three—to hearing, sight and speaking.

Perhaps this little company of Christians, well versed in God's dealings with His people as recorded in the Old Testament, would remember how God met the fearful Elijah when he had challenged the heathen Baals and fled in panic from the fury of Ahab, and from Jezebel. As he hid in a cave, the word of the Lord came to him, and said, "What doest thou here, Elijah?" (I Kings 19:9). Elijah said in answer, "I have been very jealous for the Lord, the God of hosts; for the people of Israel have forsaken thy covenant, thrown down thy altars, and slain thy prophets with the sword; and I, even I only, am left; and they seek my life, to take it away." And he said, "Go forth, and stand upon the mount before the Lord". And behold, the Lord passed by, and a great and strong wind rent the mountains, and broke in pieces the rocks before the Lord, but the Lord was not in the wind; and after the wind an earthquake, but the Lord was not in the earthquake; and after the earthquake a fire, but the Lord was not in the fire; and after the fire a still small voice. And when Elijah heard it, he wrapped his face in his mantle and went out and stood at the entrance of the cave. And behold, there came a voice to him, and said,

"What are you doing here, Elijah?" He said, "I have been very jealous for the Lord, the God of hosts; for the people of Israel have forsaken thy covenant, thrown down thy altars, and slain thy prophets with the sword; and I, even I only, am left; and they seek my life to take it away". And the Lord said to him, "Go ..." (I Kings 19:10–15 R.S.V.).

The early Christians, at most one hundred and twenty of them, united in doctrine and fellowship, were outnumbered too, but the coming of the Holy Spirit in this special experience was preliminary to the command "Go".

The Spirit's visitation was evidenced through their sense of hearing. There was "a rushing mighty wind" (v. 2). Wind is one of the symbols of the Holy Spirit. Jesus spoke to Nicodemus in these terms concerning the new life. You remember that He said to him, "Ye must be born again. The wind bloweth where it listeth, and thou hearest the sound thereof, but canst not tell whence it cometh, and whether it goeth; so is every one that is born of the Spirit". These first disciples were now given a physical experience which might confirm the spiritual validity of their new birth. God's Spirit was active in their salvation.

Again, the sense of sight contributed its evidence. They saw "cloven tongues like as of fire". Another symbol of the Holy Spirit is "fire." They were used to this symbolism, which spoke to them of God's *guidance*. As the Children of Israel made their way from the bondage of Egypt to the Promised Land, "The Lord went before them by day in a pillar of a cloud, to lead them the way; and by night in a pillar of fire, to give them light; He took not away the pillar of the cloud by day, nor the pillar of fire by night, from before the people" (Exodus 13:21, 22). They were to have this same Divine help on their journey to the Promised Land of Heaven. Often they would not know which way to turn, but the Holy Spirit had come to lighten their way and give them guidance. That is what Jesus had promised. "He will guide you into all truth" (John 16:13).

In the Old Testament, too, fire was a symbol of *purification.* I thought of this recently when I visited the smelting works at Port Pirie. The great furnaces, heated to very high temperatures, separated the small quantity of pure silver and gold from masses of ore fed into them. Malachi the prophet thought of this when he spoke of the coming of the Lord. "And He shall sit as a refiner and purifier of silver: and He shall purify the sons of Levi, and purge them as gold and silver, that they may offer unto the Lord an offering in righteousness" (Malachi 3:3). These Christians on the first Whit-Sunday needed to be purified. John the Baptist anticipated this when he said of Christ, "One mightier than I cometh, the latchet of whose shoes I am not worthy to unlose, he shall baptize you with the Holy Ghost and with fire" (Luke 3:16). So we read that cloven tongues like as of fire "sat upon each of them" (Acts 2:3). The Spirit of God was already active in their *Sanctification.*

They knew, too, the Spirit's validity as He spoke through them, and this was also a striking witness to the crowd which quickly gathered. People were amazed and said to each other, "Behold, are not all these which speak Galilaeans? And now hear we every man in our own tongues wherein we were born? Parthians, and Medes, and Elamites, and the dwellers in Mesopotamia, and in Judaea, and Cappadocia, in Pontus, and Asia,

Phrygia, and Pamphylia, in Egypt, and in the parts of Libya about Cyrene, and strangers of Rome, Jews and proselytes, Cretes and Arabians, we do hear them speak in our tongues the wonderful works of God" (vv. 7–11).

Should we as Christian believers expect to speak in tongues today? Is this an essential sign of the fulness of the Holy Spirit? There have always been Christians who have placed great emphasis upon this gift, and in recent days claims to this experience of "Glossalalia", as it is called, have been made in the larger denominations.

We must always receive with respect such claims to the gifts of the Spirit, but we must also study closely all that scripture says. St. Paul wrote to the Corinthians "Have all the gifts of healing? Do all speak with tongues? Do all interpret? But covet earnestly the best gifts: and yet shew I unto you a more excellent way ... Though I speak with the tongues of men and of angels, and have not love, I am become as sounding brass, or a tinkling symbol" (I Cor. 12:30—13:1).

He said, too, "I thank my God, I speak with tongues more than ye all: Yet in the Church I had rather speak five words with my understanding, that by my voice I might teach others also, than ten thousand words in an unknown tongue" (I Cor. 14:18–19).

Dr. Leon Morris remarks on our difficulty today in evaluating some of the gifts noted in these New Testament pages, such as "helps" and "governments" (I Cor. 12–28). "We may make conjectures ... But when we boil it all down, we know nothing about these gifts or their possession. They have vanished without leaving a visible trace." Of "tongues", he says, "Despite the confident claims of some, we cannot be certain of exactly what form the gift took in New Testament days." (*Spirit of the Living God*).

But we may be sure that whatever else "speaking in tongues" may mean today, it does mean, and always has, that God the Holy Spirit will open the mouth of the believer in the presence of others to glorify Christ to other men and women. An obedient, spirit-filled Christian is a vocally witnessing Christian. The words which he speaks are given to him by the Holy Spirit. That is what Jesus promised His disciples (Luke 12: 11–12); "When they bring you unto the synagogues, and unto magistrates, and powers, take ye no thought how or what thing ye shall answer, or what ye shall say: For the Holy Ghost shall teach you in the same hour what ye ought to say." So they had the tongues and the assurance that the Spirit of God would be active in them as they sought to serve their God and His people.

"And they were all amazed, and were in doubt, saying one to another, What meaneth this? Others mocking said, These men are full of new wine. But Peter, standing up with the eleven, lifted up his voice, and said unto them, Ye men of Judaea, and all ye that dwell at Jerusalem, be this known unto you, and hearken to my words" (Acts 2: 12–14).

Some of the crowd kept asking one another, "What does this mean?". It is wonderful when those around us begin to ask, What is it that makes you so different? Why are you so happy? You are so enthusiastic about your religion. Why? You seem able to cope with emergencies. How? When did you become a Christian? Happy is the Christian, man or woman whose non-Church-going friends begin to talk like that! They have seen what is happening in some particular Christian life, and this raises honest questions in them as to where they stand.

Of course, *witness* is double-edged. People may take notice of the Christian whose command of life impresses them: but any inconsistencies in our Christian witness will immediately be observed. Our friends may say, "I can't understand how anyone who calls himself a Christian could act like that. It looks as though there's nothing in this Christianity business after all!" But the witness of these early Christians had healthy doubts which led many who saw them, first to question their own ways, and then into transforming belief.

Others saw them with prejudiced eyes and mocked them. "These men are drunk", they said. The mockers are still active tody. You're crazy! You're airy-fairy! You're a mug! You're a religious maniac! You're a hypocrite! Mockery is one of the hardest things to endure. Ask the newly-converted footballer who witnesses amongst his team-mates, the nurse amongst the hospital staff, a businessman amongst his associates, or the schoolboy amongst his mates. Ask the born-again Christian what his family thinks, or even some of his Church friends! Christ Himself was mocked throughout His earthly ministry and above all at His trial. Was there ever mockery like this? "When they had platted a crown of thorns, they put it upon his head, and a reed in his right hand: and they bowed the knee before him, and mocked him, saying, Hail, King of the Jews!" (Matthew 27:29). That same Jesus said to all who would follow Him, "If the world hate you, ye know that it hated me before it hated you" (John 15:18), but the consistent witness of those Pentecost Christians, full indeed of new wine from the true vine of Christ Himself, brought some who mocked into true belief.

"But Peter, standing up with the eleven, lifted up his voice, and said unto them, Ye men of Judaea, and all ye that dwell at Jerusalem, be this known unto you, and hearken to my words".

This was Peter's first sermon! and it was preached in the Holy Spirit power. I know what I felt like when I preached my first sermon over twenty years ago,— and that was offered to a sympathetic and prayerful congregation. Peter spoke to a hostile, mocking, doubting crowd. But, Peter, are you justified in raising your voice like this? Your impetuosity has got you into trouble before! Didn't you make a fool of yourself in the Garden of Gethsemane, trying to stop them arresting Jesus, by striking one of the guards with a sword? You're too inconsistent as well. Didn't you profess a stronger loyalty than all the rest, before the Crucifixion? Yet when the time came you denied Christ, not once but three times. No-one will listen to you: you're inconsistent. Above all, Peter—you're plain ignorant—be realistic; you didn't have the education for a preacher. *You* haven't been trained in homiletics. You're a fisherman, not a preacher.

But the Spirit of God can make up for things like impetuosity and inconsistency, ignorance, or whatever else is lacking. Peter's witness that day was enthusiastic, expository and evangelistic.

It was—how could it be otherwise? He was filled with the Holy Spirit. It was not mere emotionalism or grim determination or exhibitionism that prompted him; it was God-given enthusiasm. So Peter's sermon was expository; he began with the Old Testament, quoting Joel, and the history of their race. He told them

124

what the purpose was of Christ's coming, His death, His Resurrection, His Ascension, His Second Coming, and the Coming of the Holy Spirit.

This great utterance was truly evangelistic and God crowned it with marvellous success. "They that gladly received his word were baptized: and the same day there were added unto them about three thousand souls. And they continued stedfastly in the apostles' doctrine and fellowship" (v.41). The Church of today faces a tremendous challenge—the unbelief, yet the utter need, of this twentieth century. What must we do to fulfil the purpose of God? The answer comes to the Church and to every individual Christian.

"Peter, standing up with the eleven, lifted up his voice" (v.14). We must each one of us witness to Christ, yet as a part of the Church and with its support. Many will doubt and mock us, but some will believe. Have you known what it is to feel yourself urged on by the Holy Spirit's power? Have you in any way at all declared your faith to others? Will you stand up for Christ and lift up your voice for Him? The fulness of the Holy Spirit is yours when you ask for it; you need no other infilling. Just let Him do His work through you. You have yourself already felt the Holy Spirit's regenerating power. He is purifying you and guiding you to your sanctification. Now let Him make you effective as you speak for Him—and as you witness to His power by upright and Christlike living.

So let us all wait upon Christ in obedience, and "with one accord".

"O Breath of Life, come sweeping through us.
Revive Thy Church with life and power;
O Breath of Life, come, cleanse, renew us,
And fit Thy Church to meet this hour".